D1025777

Other books by Marshall B. Stearn, Ph.D.

Self Hypnosis: A Method of Improving Your Life

*Drinking & Driving: Know Your Limits and Liabilities
(First Edition)*

PORTRAITS OF PASSION

Aging: Defying The Myth

BY

MARSHALL B. STEARN, Ph. D.

Park West Publishing Co.
Sausalito, California
1991

© 1991 Marshall B. Stearn, Ph. D.

Published by Park West Publishing Co.
Post Office Box 1502
Sausalito, California, 94966

All rights reserved. No part of this book may be reproduced in any form, by mimeograph or any other means, without permission in writing from the publisher.

ISBN 0-9610480-4-2

1. Biographical 2. Psychological 3. Sociological

For information contact Park West Publishing Co.
Printed in the United States of America

0 9 8 7 6 5 4 3 2 1

Dedication

In Memory Of My Dear Brother Jerry

Table Contents

Acknowledgements

Sincere thanks to Tonia Sedlock, Gwen Jones, David Steinberg, Bob Geiger, Charles Green, Barry Prager, and Paul Kleyman.

Special thanks to Computer Arts Institute of San Francisco, Lisa Atwater, and Business Works of Mill Valley.

This book could never have come about without the help and kindness of the individuals interviewed. My deepest gratitude to each and everyone of them for letting a perfect stranger come into their lives and share their personal history with him.

And finally with deep gratitude to my patient editor Terry Horne for his incisive comments, his timely wit, and his eye to detail.

Foreword

This book is a series of interviews of various people over 65 years of age. The participants are individuals from diverse personal and professional backgrounds that have made significant contributions in their respective fields, and, most notably, are still working.

The personalities involved with this project have proven to be tireless professionals who apparently defy the chronological aging myth in terms of work, productivity and creativity. My question was, "why have these individuals continued to contribute so long and so well while others have not?" This book, explores viewpoints of many different backgrounds, and from many different perspectives in an attempt to answer that question.

Reading about these individual experiences has proven to be stimulating, thought provoking, and quite possibly prototypical for present and future generations. My motivation in pursuing this project was fostered by the awareness that our population is represented by an increasing number of older Americans. I felt that we, as a nation, had to redefine and set new parameters as to what getting older really means in America. Yet, after compiling the interviews, I found what these people had to say was relevant to all ages.

Aging is universal and so far as we know it, it is not irreversible. It is a phenomenon every human being has to come to terms with: no one escapes. In reviewing the literature I found that successful aging is by no means an accident. It requires the development of lifelong habits of body and mind. The individuals I chose in my study were people who lead by example, many expressed that they were blessed by having ancestors with good genes.

The basic questions each participant was asked is as follows:

- With all you have done and accomplished why do you keep on working?
- What was in your upbringing that fostered productivity and/or creativity?
- Who were your mentor(s)?
- Is there a personal payoff for you to continue working?
- Was there a life experience(s) that effected your attitude toward life, and/or getting older?

- Has any of life's misfortunes effected your life view?
- What philosophical base do you operate from? Be it, literature, religion, psychology, philosophy, an individual, or other?
- Have you had the experience that someone (institution) thought you were less capable physically or intellectually, and how did you handle it?
- How is life different for you now as you look back?
- What advice can you give in respect to the natural phenomenon of age and work?
- Do you have any short or long-term goals? What are they, explain?
- Why do you think some people age well and others do not?
- When you're focusing on yourself, what special talent, characteristic or trait do you feel you have, and are proud of, and how has that worked for you all these years?
- While I was interviewing you, was there a question you wished I would have asked, and how would you have answered it?

The responses I received were as varied as the personalities involved. Yet, whether the information acquired through this process was curt or expansive, introspective or academic, laboriously detailed, or entertainingly anecdotal what evolved were a series of personal monographs; individual documents, as varied in expression as their authors, each testifying to the potentials and misconceptions of aging in America.

Securing well known people for interviews was relatively easy. However, it took some time and planning. There were some individuals who were just too busy with their endeavors to allow for an interview. Those who would have liked to have been interviewed, but had other pressing commitments were: Angela Lansbury, Dr. Jonas Salk, Lawrence Ferlinghetti, Former Secretary of State George Schultz, Cab Calloway, Victor Borge, Dizzy Gillespie, Isaac Stern, Milton Freidman, Dr. Armand Hammer, Walter Haas, and I. M. Pei.

Defying ageism is a strong testimony not only to the role of the creative process for older persons, but also to the necessity of creativity in every life. Alex Comfort in his book, *A Good Age*, stated that the organization of science illustrates the real and the unreal in aging folklore, and the interplay of liabilities with expectation, experience, and life cycle. Change the expectation and the life cycle and you can expect an entirely different pattern of originality, which could maintain and nurture creativity as a driving force of motivation.[1] This idea is certainly prevalent among the people who put in long hours and feel they are still at the peak of their profession: revising, synthesizing, redefining, and reevaluating their works. This principle is aptly demonstrated by the people I have interviewed.

Prologue

The first seeds of this project were planted in the 60's, when I was a high school teacher. I chaperoned the senior prom. I wore bell bottomed trousers, had a mustache, beard, long hair, and wore a big belt buckle. My date was young, beautiful and wore a mini skirt. We danced all night and enjoyed ourselves immensely. The next Monday, the students criticized me for my behavior. At that time I was in my early thirties. The students, in my opinion, were expressing the values this culture imparts that infers that adults have a responsibility to "act their age." In other words, to not engage in activities that are reserved for another generation. The students were already making determinations in terms of age, behavior, and what modern society expects of individuals as they pass through life.

It is not surprising that there is a great deal of ageism inculcated into our society through our institutions, our media, and literature. Changing those attitudes toward stereotypical behavior relative to age is a challenging task. As an example, the multi-billion dollar greeting card industry is one of the major purveyors of insidious remarks relative to the natural phenomenon of age, using birthday cards as the propaganda tool. Fairytales, passed from century to century, depict older people as ugly, sinister, and dangerous. Television commercials written by young Madison-Avenue types depict older people as fuzzy seniors, who sometimes are in a daze and dress like they had no notion of proper attire, stereotyping a group which controls over 70% of the nation's purchasing power.[2]

This is just another example that getting older is a curse. The underlying message is to know your place, and deny your own instincts. The amount of time and effort necessary to get our citizenry "up to speed" to be producers, providers, and contributors in our society through education and work experience is tremendous. So, instead of capitalizing on available resources, our society is being self-destructed by our inbred attitudes about age from early on. In other words, societal norms shoot our culture in the foot.

My personal interest in this question came about as a result of my concern for my older brother. He had lived a rather careful life, doing the right things as was expected of him by the mandates of era of which he was a part. He fought in WWII, got an honorable discharge, went to college, got a job, was deeply devoted to family, and had an extraordinary interest in psychology, religion, literature, philosophy, and classical music. He had always been into health food, drank alcohol minimally, but was a smoker. He eventually was beset with heart and lung problems and many other ailments which effected his zest for life. It was at this point that I was searching to find something which he could read and somehow give him inspiration to help himself.

It was at this time I came upon Norman Cousins' book, *Anatomy of an Illness.* I was greatly impressed with Cousins' courage and drive to find answers about his own health and body. The chapter which especially impressed me dealt with creativity. The quality of life illustrated by Pablo Casals, Verdi, Michalangelo, Picasso, and later others such as Rembrandt and Albert Schweitzer demonstrated that their creativity had been greatly enhanced when they were engaged in some activity which gave them joy which transcended their own mortality.[3] This led me into finding other books and articles about creativity, and productivity of people way beyond our society's norms. Books such as *A Fine Age: Creativity As A Key To Successful Aging*, illustrate that long-lived people are in a stage which allows their experience and resourcefulness to be expressed in a natural way.

Below are some conclusions derived from interviews by Norman M. Lobsenz of some famous people when asked why they keep working.[4]

- My work is my identity. Many derive their sense of self-esteem from what they got from their work.
- They enjoy what they do, they do only projects that interest them, getting pleasure from what they do is the motivating factor for many who no longer need to work.
- Many felt they had a creative drive that they must get out, it is the challenge to find a new idea.
- There are goals they want to accomplish. A drive that will not allow the individuals to quit if they feel they can make a contribution.
- They got emotional rewards as a payoff. There was a sense of satisfaction from a job well done.
- Work is the mainspring of life, a natural driving force expressing the human characteristic of doing something, whether it be constructive or not.

I decided to go into depth about the intrinsic factors relative to my interviewee's background, upbringing, and influential experiences.

Many of the participants had never put their feelings on these issues into words, and thus the interview process provided a means for clarifying to themselves some of the questions posed to them.

It is my hope that these interviews will be inspirational and illuminating to people of all ages. Hopefully the text will serve as a reminder of our own possibilities for living long, well, and productively. Young people today have a greater promise of long life than previous generations. A boy born in the 1980's can expect to live to the age of 70 plus, a girl to the age of 77 plus. Keeping in mind that these estimates are of average life expectancy, they imply that millions of children with above average chances will live into their eighties and nineties and beyond.

There is clear evidence that today's young people, on the whole, have a negative view of aging and very stereotyped ideas about what it means to be old. Teenagers may look forward to the time when they enjoy certain privileges of adulthood and establish their own independence and identity, but they definitely do not look forward to be being middle-aged or old. In this they share the general cultural bias of our society in favor of youth and youthfulness.

For the first time in our history, the number of Americans over 65 is higher than the number of those under 19. Our fastest growing group is the 30,000,000 people over 65. In 1900, only 1 out of 25 Americans was over the age of 65, today it is 1 out of 8, by 2020 it will be 1 out of 5. In 1985, there were 2.9 millions over 85, by the year 2020, there will be 7.3 million. In 1900, about the time that the grandparents of today's high school students were born, life expectancy was only forty-seven years. Since that time the population of the United States has tripled, but the population of people over sixty-five has grown seven times--equivalent to the combined population of our twenty one smallest states.[5]

According to Sula Benet, a professor of Anthropology at Hunter College of New York, in an article from, *Aging Annual,* "Not long ago, in the village of Tamish in the Soviet Republic of Abkhasia," he said, "I raised my glass of wine to toast a man who looked no more than 70, I said, 'May you live as long as Moses (120),' He was not pleased. He was 119." Dr. Benet studied Abkhasian culture for an extended period of time and has consulted with the Academy of Sciences of USSR, the Ethnographic Institute in the City of Sukhumi, and the Institute of Gerontology in Sukhumi. These were his conclusions:

> *The Abkhasians live as long as they do primarily because of the extraordinary cultural factors that*

structure their existence: the uniformity and certainty
of both individual and group behavior, the unbroken
continuum of life's activities, the same games, the same
work, the same food, the same self imposed and socially
perceived needs. And the important increasing prestige
that comes with getting older.[6]

If we leave learning about aging and the aged to the disorganized and often biased input from the media in the form of jokes, cartoons, skits, and popular myths we will be doing a disservice to young people and a country that will have one-half of its population over fifty very soon. Young people will learn about aging whether we teach them or not, but what they learn may be false and harmful. The longevity revolution has immense repercussions for all aspects of society. Tax structures, allocation of resources, production and marketing, family, religion, careers, retirement, housing, entertainment, education, law, medical care, and scientific research are among the areas being affected. As a result aging has become everybody's business.

According to Understanding Aging, Inc., the vast influence of the longevity revolution is occurring in an America which is ill-prepared for it. Americans have mixed feelings about aging, and the negative attitudes often dominate the way we think about long life and behavior toward older people. Widespread myths and misinformation foster age prejudice and discrimination. This negativity creates a poor foundation for confronting the many issues emerging in our aging society.[7] Researchers can now demonstrate that certain crucial areas of human intelligence do not decline in old age among people who are generally healthy. The new research challenges beliefs held long by scientists, and suggests that among people who remain physically and emotionally healthy some of the most important forms of intellectual growth can continue well into the 80's. The "use or lose it" principle applies not only to the maintenance of muscular flexibility, but to the maintenance of high levels of intellectual performance.[8]

As we age, many of us encounter crises of various kinds: deaths of loved ones, involuntary changes in economic status, and residences. The question arises -- what enables some people to bounce back from such situations while others are seriously disabled by the same kinds of experiences? Robert L. Kahn, Ph.D., program director of the Institute for Social Research at the University of Michigan states that there is evidence that people who receive social support from family and friends after surgery recover more quickly than others. He further states that there must be a combination of genetic factors, personality, and social factors that enable and encourage such resilience. But, he says, we don't know what all these factors are or how they combine.

The dominate view of aging in our culture is that it is a time of inevitable decrements and losses. For some people, however, the experience of age produces a quality of judgement or wisdom that they didn't have in younger years. Kahn states, "Our research has neglected exploring the positive aspects of aging and the factors that will evoke these qualities and encourage their expression."

In many cases, in later years people are no longer dependent on society in the same way as they were earlier in their lives. They have climbed the company ladder, have become their own bosses, have become successful, and have retired. A person who lives in a society which considers older people useless and expendable is likely to have a negative view on his/her own aging. Conversely a person who lives in a society which looks upon older people as wise and useful citizens worthy of respect is likely to have positive feelings about their own aging.[9]

The social-psychological view of aging is one which considers personality to be the most critical factor in determining how a person adapts during the later years. It follows that people will likely approach aging in much the same ways they approach other phases of their lives. In other words, a somewhat assertive middle-aged person is likely to continue to be assertive with age. A person who withdraws in young and middle adulthood is likely to become even more noticeably withdrawn. The implications here relate to how a person develops early on, how they deal with life's bumpy road, as to whether their later years will be successful, productive happy, creative, or not.[10]

PART ONE

Family, Diversity,
and Personal Motivation

Linus Pauling

CHAPTER ONE

Linus Pauling

Linus Pauling was born in Portland, Oregon on February 28, 1901, and was educated in Oregon (B.S. in Chemical Engineering, Oregon Agricultural College, 1922) and California (Ph.D., California Institute of Technology, 1925). He was a member of the teaching staff of the California Institute of Technology from 1922 to 1963; Research Professor of the Physical and Biological Sciences with the Center for the Study of Democratic Institutions, Santa Barbara, California from 1963 to 1967; Professor of Chemistry at the University of California, San Diego from 1967 to 1969; Professor of Chemistry at Stanford University, 1969 to 1973 (now Professor Emeritus); and Research Professor, Linus Pauling Institute of Science and Medicine, 1973 to present.

In 1948, Pauling was awarded the Presidential Medal for Merit *by President Truman. He received the 1954 Nobel Prize in Chemistry for his research on the nature of the chemical bond in relation to the structure of complex substances, and he was awarded the Nobel Peace Prize for 1962 for his commitment to nuclear disarmament.*

Dr. Pauling has published over 650 scientific papers, nearly 200 articles on social and political issues, and over a dozen books ranging from The Structure of Line Spectra *to* How to Live Longer and Feel Better. *He has received honorary doctorates by some forty-five universities, and scores of other honors too numerous to mention.*

———❖———

Portraits of Passion: Aging, Defying the Myth

From my earliest years I found pleasure in understanding things. Also, for some reason, when I first started through school I got the idea that getting a grade of 90 percent was hardly satisfactory, that one ought to get a grade of 100 percent. I wanted to understand clearly everything that was being presented to me. My father had some influence on me, correcting me somewhat in scientific matters, but he died when I was 9 years old. When I was 12, I began studying minerals. At 13, I became interested in chemistry. A boy my own age showed me some chemical reactions in his own home. I was entranced by these chemical reactions--substances being converted into other substances, so I got out my father's chemistry textbook and read it. Two years later I had a course in high-school chemistry and it was clear that this was my field.

When I was fifteen, my grandmother asked me, "Liney, what are you going to be when you grow up?" I said, "I'm going to be a chemical engineer." I didn't know that there were professional chemists, but I knew about chemical engineering. When I was sixteen I worked in a machine shop. My salary was increased every payday, I think simply because I was completely reliable. The salary got to be enough that my mother felt I should continue working in the machine shop and not go to college. I had been giving my salary to her, to be returned to me when I went to college. I needed to stand up to my mother and say that I was going. So I did.

At the end of my sophomore year, I managed to get a job as paving plant inspector with the State of Oregon. The Chemistry Department of the Oregon Agricultural College sent me a telegram offering me a job as assistant instructor at $100 a month. So I accepted that and for nearly the rest of the academic year I taught the sophomore chemistry courses in quantitative analysis.

At Oregon Agricultural College, there was one man who influenced many students. He was professor of chemical engineering, and was an enthusiast about graduate work. There were very few people on the staff of the college who had doctor's degrees. He felt that the doctor's degree was very important. He managed to get seven of the fourteen graduates in chemical engineering to go off to graduate school.

I had much curiosity about the world. What I wanted to do was learn more about the nature of the universe. Fortunately I was able to start doing this immediately after I became a graduate student, answering some questions that I myself had formulated about why different substances have different properties. Then, I liked finishing a job, and to me finishing a job in research investigation consists in bringing it to the point where it is published. When the discovery is published, then I feel satisfied. I have a good memory. I remember very well the things I am interested in remembering, scientific things. I have a sense of responsibility in that I believe in doing jobs, getting things done. It's more than a job well done. It is an interesting job well done that satisfies my curiosity and should satisfy other people's curiosity. Then there's a quality I judge that I have which I can express by quoting something said by one of my students at my sixty-fifth birthday party. He had asked me, about thirty years earlier, "Dr. Pauling, how do you get good ideas?" I said, "You have a lot of ideas and throw away the bad ones." So, I have the capability of having lots of ideas. This often involves cross connections between different aspects of my memory banks--different fields of knowledge. I seem to have good judgment in throwing away the bad ones and not wasting time on problems I'm not going to be able to solve.

When we were married in 1923, my wife decided that her job was to see that I was not distracted from my course of thinking about scientific problems. So for many years she tried to protect me from being distracted by taking care of all the problems that arose. I'm reminded of the story of the man who said that he and his wife had made an agreement in which she would decide all of the minor problems and he would decide the major ones, and so far there hadn't been any major problems.

I'm fortunate in that I've been all of my life about half an experimental scientist and half a theoretical scientist. Much of my experimental work I'm no longer able to continue, but I can continue with my theoretical work just as I have in the past. There are genetic and environmental factors that determine how well the brain continues to function. I think the nutritional factors are very strong in this matter. I was lucky in that I became interested in vitamins twenty-five years ago, in 1965, and that my megavitamin regimen since then has helped me to keep mentally active and alert.

The work on vitamins and health that I am doing now on using vitamins and minerals in an attempt to control diseases is not so interesting to me scientifically as work on other problems. I do this work largely because I feel that it is important. When my book *Vitamin C and the Common Cold* came out I was astonished. The medical profession jumped on me! I thought they would be happy to have some control of that disease, which is such a nuisance. Most of it is a bias that they have developed early, the physicians, the medical authorities, and the nutritional authorities, against the idea that vitamins in large doses have value. This bias is very hard to get rid of. Fred Stare of the Harvard School of Public Health said in his review of my book, "Dr. Pauling has never had a course in nutrition, so how can he talk about it?" Well, I've never had a course in biochemistry, I was looking over a book that had the phrase, "Dr. Pauling, the famous biochemist ...". I don't think of myself as a biochemist, but the biochemists in general do think of me as a biochemist.

The population of the earth has increased greatly during my lifetime. There have been tremendous changes in the world. It is coming close to the point where the quality of life will deteriorate unless there is control of the population. The quality of life is good for a small fraction of the earth's people and pretty poor for others. It's been twenty years perhaps since I gave some lectures on the subject in New Delhi. Since then I've been saying that we should strive to have a world in which every human being is capable of leading a good life. We are far from that now. When I was a boy back about 1910 there were a few people who were talking about preserving the environment, conservation. We haven't made enough progress in that direction. There are too many people who work to increase the number of people.

For example, I received a document from a distinguished physician saying that if everyone were to become a vegetarian we could support many more billions of people on Earth because it is wasteful to pass corn and grain through animals which we then eat. I don't think that's the goal, to have the maximum number of people leading poorer lives. We should have whatever number of people the earth can support leading good lives. I no longer worry about the destruction of civilization through nuclear war. We should be attacking the problem of population.

My goal at the present time is to continue to be as happy as I can. That consists in putting most of my time and effort into obtaining a greater understanding of the world through my discoveries. I publish more papers now than I ever did before. Part of the reason is that up until twenty years ago I was spending a good bit of my time teaching and some time as an administrator. And of course, much of my time is working for world peace, control of nuclear weapons, radioactive fallout, and so on. I still spend some time on these various problems, but I have more time to attack scientific problems than ever before. The problems I attack are, first, those I think I can solve, rather than problems that have a great impact on the world.

All of my life I've been able to take pleasure in making discoveries and learning something new about the world, not just learning something new, but finding something new. In the case of people who have followed some profession or business, when they've retired, conditions may be such that it's no longer possible for them to carry on the same sort of activity. A businessman can't be active unless he has a business.

Hanna Fromm

CHAPTER TWO

Hanna Fromm

Hanna Fromm has been committed to higher education all her life. In the mid 1970's she pioneered with her husband the founding and funding of the Fromm Institute for Lifelong Learning at the University of San Francisco, and became its executive director. The institute daily instructs retirees from ages 50-93 on issues which help keep them informed and active, and provides a catalyst for their energies and abilities.

Hanna Fromm was born in Nurnberg, Germany. She received her degree in Choreography and Music at the Folkwang School at the University of Essen, Germany. She later continued her education in France and England. Living in San Francisco since 1941, Hanna Fromm has served on many boards such as the National Council on the Aging, The American Red Cross, The Community Music Center, Geriatric Curriculum Program Board of the University of California San Francisco Medical Center, and the National Board of Fine Arts Museum. For her innovative work she was awarded an honorary degree of Doctor of Public Service *from the University of San Francisco. Hanna received the* Living Legend Award *at the International Women's Center in San Diego, California. She has formerly held active director's positions with Amnesty International, Legal Aid to the Elderly, and the National Council on Aging. Hanna and her husband have a son, a daughter, and 5 grandchildren.*

———— ❖ ————

Portraits of Passion: Aging, Defying the Myth

First of all, I enjoy productive work. It keeps me alive. I know I'm needed here. I've never been a passionate housewife who goes around cleaning all day, neither do I enjoy ladies' luncheons; I've want to do something worthwhile and make a contribution to society.

I come from a family of learned people. My father was a doctor, a poet, and a violinist. My mother and my whole family were well educated. My own life, however, took a different direction from my family's as I did not choose academia, but rather dance, music, choreography, and teaching.

My father died when I was thirteen, and both my mother and I were devastated. From then on, I was more or less on my own and had to take care of my mother. In 1932, I left Germany to continue school in England. Hitler came to power 1933 and I never went back home.

My early mentors were my father and mother, and the many scholarly friends of my parents. I have traveled a lot and lived, studied, and worked in London, Paris, and Jerusalem.

The Fromm Institute for Lifelong Learning which is now in existence for 15 years gives me great satisfaction. Its structure is something I have developed more or less on my own, but, along with the help of many professional educators. Before that, I was a mother and a helpmate to my husband, his large family, and his extensive business life.

As a child, I never liked older people, but actually I was afraid of what they represented. The wrinkles, pains, the physical decline of old people frightened me. And now that I'm older myself, I'm still frightened. I finally asked myself why don't you do something, not only to keep other people my age vital, alive, and active, and myself too. I got started in academia late in life since I have no training in the workings of a university, it was a very hard and difficult beginning with many sleepless nights. But I have learned and it shows you that you can teach an old dog new tricks.

Because of my father's death and Hitler's rise to power, I had many unfulfilled dreams. I never became the physician I wanted to be. But here I am at my age doing something I believe in, something important and meaningful. I am very grateful for this chance.

I don't think I have ever been discriminated against because of my age, nor because I am a woman, nor have I been discouraged from doing what I felt I must do.

My present active life is fulfilling. As we get older, the future is a bit frightening, I sometimes get scared and depressed like everybody else. But I have a husband who is a very positive thinker, my husband doesn't want to indulge in those feelings. I am fortunate that I have a lifelong mate with whom to share my innermost thoughts and feelings, and I'm blessed with caring children and grandchildren.

Work is not necessarily everybody's need, but I feel people should stay intellectually, emotionally alive, be curious, and not stay home and watch television. Interaction with people is very important.

The Fromm Institute requires a lot of work, but it's something I like to do. It took two years of research to get the concept of the institute established. Seventeen years ago, I was sick for several months and had time to talk to a lot of friends. And I found out how many retired people were lonely, felt unneeded, and missed structured and constructive life.

Retired professors suffer the same trauma of retirement as other people. Many find out that they miss teaching and interacting with students. A cousin of mine who taught at Harvard, was looking forward to retirement, so he could devote his time to writing. Yet, he became severely depressed after retirement and could not write till other universities asked him to be a guest lecturer. He is now 87 years old, and is still an active author.

A banker friend of ours said to me one day, "Can you imagine six months ago, I was somebody and now I feel I am nothing. Nobody calls me and asks for my advice. And the few consulting jobs I have are not fulfilling." He died after two years and research shows that many simply die after they have stopped working and life losses meaning for them unless they are prepared to keep their minds busy.

I asked my husband, "What would you do if you had to retire?" His prompt answer was, "I hope I never retire, but if I had to, I would like to go back to the university and study all of the things I never had time for. But, I don't want to study with my grandchildren, nor do I want to be taught by professors who could be grandchildren of mine, but by people of my own age group who have had much the same life experience." My husband is 85 years old and is still working full days at the office.

The institute leaves me very little time for myself, but I feel it is my responsibility to see that it is successful, that it expands and grows intellectually. We are fortunate that we have an extremely capable director and an outstanding academic advisor. Now in its 15th year, we have 40 faculty and 500 students who are all retired.

My work keeps me stimulated and gives me a purpose in life. I had to develop talents that I never knew I had and hope to keep on going as long as my health permits.

I don't know why some people age better than others, maybe it's genes or good medical care combined with a positive attitude. My hope is to stay healthy and vital so I can be of use to my family, my community, and that I have the privilege of enjoying my grandchildren.

Joan Bekins, Photographer

Elizabeth Terwilliger

CHAPTER THREE

Elizabeth Terwilliger

California naturalist Elizabeth Cooper Terwilliger is a trail blazer in the world of conservation and environmental education. A resident of Marin County, she has effectively campaigned for more bicycle paths, the preservation of marshes, coastal land, and wooded areas that have been the home of the Monarch Butterfly for years untold. She helped to obtain the land for the National Audubon Society's Richardson Bay Wildlife Sanctuary in Tiburon, California where she initiated an outdoor education program.

Mrs. Terwilliger was born in 1909, the daughter of a physician on a sugar plantation. She grew up in Hawaii, graduating from Punahou and the University of Hawaii. She received her M.A. from Columbia University and her R.N. from Stanford University School of Nursing.

In 1975, the Terwilliger Nature Education Center in Marin County, California, which teaches children an awareness and appreciation of Nature and wildlife, was created by volunteers to expand and perpetuate her work. Her tactile teaching methods have been praised around the world through her five Tripping with Terwilliger habitat films. Each year, three hundred prints are used by 15,000 teachers nationwide and viewed by about one million children. She received the John Muir Award at the National Education Film Festival in 1975 for Grassland, Chaparral, and the CINE Golden Eagle Award for the film Bay Tidelands in 1973.

Elizabeth was honored by the San Francisco Examiner in 1972 as one of the Bay Area's "Ten Most Distinguished Citizens". In 1984, President Reagan honored her with the Volunteer Action Award. Two years later Robert Redford presented her with the Chevron Conservation Award.

Portraits of Passion: Aging, Defying the Myth

Newsweek named her as one of 1988's American Heroes
Award recipients.
  Elizabeth is a widow and has two children and three
grandsons.[11]

———— ❖ ————

My mother was a teacher. She had us all reading out loud when
we were young. There were three of us, two older brothers and myself.
We used to take turns reading and she would pronounce and interpret
the words that we didn't know. We'd look them up in the dictionary.
Things we read about were of other parts of the world. I grew up on
a sugar plantation and we didn't have any of the things that we read
about. We read Ernest Thompson Seton's *Wild Animals I Have Known.*
We didn't have any of those wild animals in the islands. Reading was
an adventure, I could use my imagination.

As a little girl on the plantation I was exposed to many of the people
that lived there and worked there. They came from Scotland, from
England, from Ireland, from France, Portugal, Philippines, Spain and
India. They came from all over the world, and we were with people
who had all different backgrounds. I really had a rich upbringing.

I learned if something had to be done, I did not wait for it to be
done, I would try to do something about it. Later on in my adult life
I would go to city council meetings, planning commissions and boards
of supervisors. Those meetings are better than any movie or any TV
show, because it's like the stage. It's like a play, only it's for real. If you
persevere you can enact change.

If you're going to spend your life helping somebody, you want to
do something that they will appreciate. So I decided to become a nurse.
I selected the Stanford School of Nursing's three-year course in San
Francisco, and to get there I went all the way around the world on boat,
train, and plane from Honolulu. I always appreciated every experience.
We were given three weeks vacation our first year. I decided to go to
Yosemite. In the morning I hiked with a ranger naturalist and in the
afternoon I hiked with a different ranger naturalist, and in the evening
there was a ranger naturalist program. Then for a whole week I and
other hikers went in the back country with a ranger/naturalist. These
were wonderful learning experiences for me in the out-of-doors.

It's important to help people. Find something that you enjoy doing.

Don't do something that you don't want to do; do something your whole spirit loves to do. Find something exciting that you can share with others.

Many older people just sit by their windows. You see them sitting by their windows looking out. I take stuffed animals and birds to retirement homes and let them hold them on their laps. They say, "I remember on the ranch, I remember on the farm." And just watching their faces light up is rewarding.

I do not want to miss anything, and I don't want other people to miss anything. There's so much out there to see, to touch, to feel, to smell. I want to show somebody else what they missed. I want to continue to teach everyone about the out-of-doors, to make them aware of it, to teach others to love and protect the out-of-doors. *You don't want to miss anything.* When you're busy in the out-of-doors, you don't have time to get old!

Below is an excerpt of an article entitled, "Life with Elizabeth" written by Calvin Terwilliger M.D., in honor of his wife's 80th birthday in the Terwilliger Center's newsletter, *The Pelican*, May 1989.

Marriage is complex, and, beside the essential ingredients of love and bliss, other factors contribute to its longevity. Mutual recognition of equality results in continuous confusion as to who is the fox and who is the hunter, and the joyous chase continues.

Elizabeth knew much more about Mother Nature's other children than I, and the sun was brighter when she was there. The walks were all too few, but led into a land of enchantment, and became addictive. There was little money and no car. Dedication and work ethic demanded "full time and best effort," and it was difficult at times to find a substitute intern to sign out so we could have time off together from the hospital. There were minor obstacles, and there was no complaint.

The scientific nature of our walks gradually changed from study of diverse species to more local consideration of one species: homo sapiens. The academic year was ending, and it was suddenly apparent to me that termination of my association with Elizabeth would be intolerable.

Editor's Note: The Terwilligers shared 50 years of marriage.

Dave Brubeck

CHAPTER FOUR

Dave Brubeck

© 1990 David W. Brubeck.

Jazz musician/composer/performer David Warren Brubeck was born in Concord, California on Dec. 6, 1920. He received his B.A. from the College of the Pacific, did graduate work in composition at Mills College, and in the course of his career has garnered honorary doctorates from University of the Pacific, Fairfield University, University of Bridgeport, Mills College, and Niagara University.

Brubeck formed the legendary Dave Brubeck Quartet in 1951; a band which toured the world introducing Brubeck's individual style and unusual musical perspective to audiences ranging from jazz clubs to symphonic concert halls. The group earned praise in the period from 1952- 1955 by topping jazz polls conducted by Downbeat, Melody Maker, Cashbox, Billboard, *and* Playboy.

Brubeck's musical vision has led him during the course of his career into a variety of expressive forms including ballet (Points on Jazz. Four Brubeck Pieces.), *orchestral works* (Elementals. They All Sang Yankee Doodle.), *the Mass* (To Hope), *and twelve other major choral works with orchestra; in addition to over two hundred jazz compositions including the classic* In Your Own Sweet Way, *and* Blue Rondo a la Turk.

Dave Brubeck has received numerous awards: among them the B.M.I. Jazz Pioneer Award in 1985, the Compostela Humanitarian Award in 1986, the American Eagle Award

Portraits of Passion: Aging, Defying the Myth

of the National Music Council in 1988, and the Gerald Manley Hopkins Award in 1990. He was named a Duke Ellington Fellow at Yale University, and Officier de L'Ordres des Arts et des Lettres in France.

Dave Brubeck is married and has six children.

————— ❖ —————

In the case of my friends, all of us, my age younger or older, we much prefer to work. I've seen it over and over again. Every year when we go to Europe, you'll see the older guys sitting there, so glad they made the tour. I often think of the nomadic tribes. That when you're so old, and you get to a certain river and you can't get across, you stay on the other side, and the tribe goes on without you. The herd, even your dogs want to stay with you, but they obey and leave you. You're left there. So when we go to Europe, year after year, we kind of look and see who made it across the pond to make that tour. This year, I was sitting in Nice with the person that put together the tour, George Wein. He remarked that B.B. King was out of the hospital and had made the tour. Cab Calloway was there, and Lionel Hampton. They're still making the crossing. And then there's the kids coming up that want to see how the older guys play and work and you pass on the tradition from one to the other.

My father was a cattle man. He had artery problems. They told my dad that the worst possible thing he could do was to ride horseback. So we used to get after him because he'd be riding all day long. He would say, "I have to go out this way. I want to go out doing what I've loved to do all my life." I think about that all the time, because that's the way he went out. He'd ridden all day the day before he died, and he was going to get up and ride all the next day. All my life I saw his work habits. He managed a 45 thousand acre ranch, and his work habits were part of me.

My mother, being a musician, was just the same. She usually taught all day long, and then practice at night. They were both so totally absorbed in what they were doing. She taught till I guess she was in her mid 60's.

My mentors were my mother and father and my brothers. I actually studied with my brother, Howard, at Mills College when he was Darius

Milhaud's assistant. My brother Henry's band rehearsed in our home, so I heard his jazz band from the time I was, say, 5 or 6. But both brothers were a tremendous influence on me.

Duke Ellington was my professional mentor. Now there's a guy with work habits. We would tour by train in the old days, Duke didn't like to fly. He would compose and write music usually late at night. He loved to write on trains. That way you didn't waste your time.

My other mentor was Darius Milhaud. Even in a social gathering if he got an idea he could listen to the conversation, know everything's that going on, and at the same time be writing music. It was phenomenal. He worked constantly.

I know that it's a very positive thing for me to play a performance. This week, I've just come home from touring and playing. We toured all over Europe, places like Turkey and Finland, Italy, France, and the Netherlands. I have a tremendous desire to live on. I have so many commissions ahead to write that I really don't have a free minute. The only trouble with that is, that every day is like finals week: a lot of pressure. And those commissions with a deadline, where there's going to be an audience sitting there and I have agreed to have the music ready, not just on opening night but months before, because it has to be rehearsed by a chorus and the parts copied. Those continuous deadlines are the one thing that I wish I didn't have. I wish I could work without them, but that's part of the business.

I would say World War II was an experience about life that sobered me up in a hurry. I was in the war. I lost a lot of friends in it. I saw firsthand the destruction of cities, so that I couldn't believe that I survived it. I still remember it almost every day. There'll be something that will make me remember how devastating that war was to my generation. Life had a new meaning for me after that experience.

I am very aware of the similarity between all great religions. There was one sentence that really made me ponder and think. Christ saying, "Love your enemy, do good to those that hate you." Buddha, 600 years before Christ, had said, "The crowning enlightenment is to love your enemy." If we are to survive it is an attitude which the world must come to. Politics, religion, and reality sometimes don't mesh. The greatness of that sentence, "love your enemies" is that it acknowledges that you will have enemies. It's so practical and so real. And you've got to accept that you're always going to have conflict.

Once in a while somebody will say to me, "Why are you still

performing at your age? Don't you find it hard?" I'll say, "If you were with me for the last six weeks, you'd have to agree that it is an endurance test." When I was a kid I was around so many old cowboys that I couldn't keep up with. I think of them when some of the younger musicians can't keep up with me. I've known guys that worked into their 90's as cowboys and they're like a piece of iron, working in weather that the average man would say is inhuman. Honest to goodness, it's unbelievable the toughness of some of these older guys that I knew.

I think that aging well is a matter of chance. You never know what virus you're going to pick up. What you inherit from the minute you're born, the genetic factor, how much oxygen got to your brain the first few minutes you lived. Things you have no control over. That's why you must be sympathetic to everyone. "There, but for the grace of God, go I."

I think that I'm playing better and writing better now. I feel that I'm running out of time, not creativity. So I try to take advantage of what time I have and work as hard as I can. Things that I want to say, as in my choral works and my sacred works, are important to me. And it's also important to my family to know that this is what I think. But it has to first satisfy me. If it carries over to the public, that's great.

I wanted to be a composer from the time I was maybe five years old. I had abilities, but certain things did not come easy to me. Writing music was one. I still fight it a little. I would say that my philosophy is like that of the old ball player Satchel Page, "Never look back, something might be gaining on you." Sometimes I think, oh, I'll never get there, but I keep trying.

Beatrice Wood

CHAPTER FIVE

Beatrice Wood

Potter, ceramicist, artist, photographer, author, lover of life and art, these words barely sketch a portrait of the world-famous and recognized virtuoso Beatrice Wood. Born in San Francisco on March 3, 1893, she has studied with Gertrud and Otto Natzler of Los Angeles, attended Finch School of New York and the Academie Julien, Paris. Beatrice has won many awards and has had numerous exhibitions in noted museums around the world. The artist was declared a California Treasure in 1984.

Her ceramics are displayed in the Smithsonian Institute, Metropolitan Museum of Art in New York and other international museums. She is renowned for her rare and beautiful luster glazes, and her often blithe and humorous depiction of women and men. She has also authored the book I Shock Myself, *her autobiography.*

Historians of Modern Art may recall her close connection with artist Marcel DuChamp (Nude Descending the Staircase), *and author Henri-Pierre Roche* (Jules and Jim). *Today, Beatrice Wood is a significant artistic force in her own right.*

Living in Ojai, California, she does the work she loves brilliantly and with passion. At 97, Beatrice Wood works everyday at her art. She is prolific, imaginative, always seeking new and different art forms to express her profound feelings for the joy of life and living. Her expansive and extraordinary works seem to both symbolize and realize the mind of the artist.

Portraits of Passion: Aging, Defying the Myth

Her most frequently quoted remark is her answer to the question, "To what do you attribute your longevity?" Her usual answer without hesitation is: "Curiosity, chocolates, and younger men."[12]

Many of us, perhaps all of us, have passion when we can relate to the things we like. I have often said that if I had to run an elevator, which to me is stopping every few minutes, that would be a most awful occupation. I'd think to myself, I don't care. You see, if I had to do anything that I didn't like, I would just let go of it.

I think I was born creative. I'm very "eye-minded". I was remembering the other day how visual things would titillate my imagination, so it was very natural for me to grow into art. My parents did not allow for my creativity to develop. They were loving, they spoiled me. They brought me up with great comfort, but that was not what I wanted. My mother got in the way of my desires for creativity. So, finally I left home with $15 and I had one beautiful "hell of a time." I chose it and I would chose it again. And through the months and years that I had no money, I touched what life was about. Now at this venerable age of almost being 100, I know a little bit about what it is to be alive. I know that gold-plated plumbings are not the answer to happiness and that's a great thing to learn.

My family brought me up to be a rose pedal on a down cushion, they thought I was unable to do anything practical. They wanted me to marry a stockbroker. It was very hard for me to learn how to earn a living. I have a soulful, dreamy temperament. It was very hard for me to jump into the world without any money and find myself. I didn't know what it was all about. Now, I think my friend, Reagan, says people don't want to work and so forth. I don't agree with this point of view. I agree with his charm but not his point of view about humanity.

Life is entirely different for me now. My life has changed so completely, as if I am another person. From being a soulful, dreamy person, now I'm very accurate, very clear, very business-like about relationships with people. I see the importance of being absolutely honest with all our relationships. But I don't think a woman should ever be absolutely honest with a man, because that's not fun. Years ago a friend said that you don't know what a relationship is like till you have it with your own sex, because there is such understanding. And I said yes, but the fascination of the masculine and feminine is that they don't exactly meet, so there is always a little thing that makes it very fascinating. I think a woman is never, this is speaking in a very sulking way, completely honest with a man, or a man with a woman. Thank God. It gives a little spice to life

I think it very important that people to be able to fall in love. If your heart is broken you learn something more about what life is like. You learn a lot about yourself. I think love is a very basic thing. The process of falling in love is not really love. One is lucky if love is involved with it. But the process itself is a most mysterious, enchanting, emotional involvement. And I think it's a great experience certainly for a woman and I think it should be that for a woman. Love enlightens and enhances one's life.

I'm very interested in philosophy. I don't like to proselytize. I became a theosophist 63 years ago. It is not a religion, I don't know how to define it. From what I understand, the only thing about being a theosophist is you recognize the oneness of the Human Race and have a feeling of brotherhood. This interests me very much. It is to study relative religions. It's opened me to all kinds of literature, ideas, all kinds of possible explanations of the beginning of the universe. I have learned so much being associated with these philosophical thoughts.

I'm not concerned with getting older. I don't think about it, that is not a problem. I have said to all the world that I'm 97, but to me I'm 32 and I'm not concerned. My very dear friend Rosalind always playfully says that we're old, "Beatrice, at your age, you shouldn't..." I don't think like that. I've never thought that way. I just have a good time. Today if I pick up the paper and begin reading and then see that the person is 85, oh my God. I turn to something else. So I'm unreasonable. I don't like old people. I'm not connected with it. It is unreasonable, but life's unreasonable.

Some people have a natural aggressiveness that they can use in the most awful circumstances and lift themselves out. If the person thinks in a certain direction and has energy, they can get out of their own prison. If they have a certain kind of personality, they can reach their goals and change things. Even people who we may think are just nobodies, they get into some crisis and they'll be heros. They'll give their life to save another person. So we really don't know what is the human potential.

I think if one has an activity that one loves whether it is cooking, painting, or building a bridge, there is no limit as to when to stop. It's different, for instance, if you are a wife, your children grow up, leave, your husband dies and your activity has gone from you. But with me, all I have to bother about is the clay. There is no reason why I shouldn't keep on. My eyes are full of ideas, so I keep on working. It's absolutely a joy for me. If I had an occupation that I didn't like, certainly I would have stopped at 65 and just vegetated, but I love what I'm doing. It's a passion with me.

I see no reason why one shouldn't work until one cannot work anymore. I'm only 3 years away from being 100, which is indecent. It's obscene to think of me ever being 100. Obscene, you know, but there are people who are 100 still working. So it's an individual thing. The mind is separate from the body. Of course, if the body doesn't behave at all then the mind can't function. You see the mind weakens with the body, that's a different thing.

I'm ready to die. Often when I'm very tired, my heart slows down and I think, "Oh, this is it." But then I revive because I have desire, desire to make the things that are in my mind. This is life. But if I don't have it, my God, I can't wait to get back to my workroom and do what I have in my mind. Desire is the mischief maker. Desire keeps us alive. The thing is as one grows older not to put water on people's desire, but to open the door so that it can still bloom a little bit.

I really want to be an honest, compassionate person. Greater than my interest in pottery is my awareness of the human frailties. I am very aware of my violence, violence that we all have. All great teachers have directed men to know themselves. That can have great meaning if you face it. We don't face it. If I know that I'm overcome with greed, with ambition, I can't stop till I face what I am. If I see I'm petty, full of impatience, I can't stop until I'm willing to face it and let it go.

Robert Mondavi

CHAPTER SIX

Robert Mondavi

Robert Gerald Mondavi was born June 18, 1913 in Virginia, Minnesota. He graduated from Stanford University with a major in Economics. In 1937, he began working for the Mondavi Family wine business known as the Sunnyhill Winery in St. Helena, California. The name was later changed to the Sunny St. Helena Winery. In 1943, the family bought 100 vine acres of Charles Krug Winery and soon after replanted the vineyards to the finest varietals. In 1957, under the Charles Krug label, they started to distribute premium wines to the east. He was the first Napa Valley vintner to utilize cold fermentation extensively in the wine making process. He also introduced blind tasting in the Napa valley. A trip to Europe had him change the size and quality of barrels the wine was to age in, which helped produced high quality wines.

He is involved in such projects as a joint venture with the Rothschild family. He is a member of the University of California - Davis Board of Visitors, and a founder of the American Institute of Wine and Food. He was International Wine and Spirits Competition Winemaker of the Year in 1982. He served on the Advisory Council of the American Conference of Chefs, and has many other honors to his credit for his innovative work. At 77, he still works daily at the winery.

———— ❖ ————

Well frankly, I've been wanting to transfer the business for the last five years and give the entire responsibility over to my children, and to what I call my extended family in the winery. I've kept working

Portraits of Passion: Aging, Defying the Myth

beyond because we had to go on an international basis with the business. I wanted to act as only a consultant, an advisor. I find that now I'm going to try to transfer this whole thing completely over to them, while they make up their minds just how this ought to be run. In the meantime, I just want them to come to me to talk, to hear what I have to say. I will always be a consultant. I'd like to be that, if they can use me.

I want to slow down too, to be very honest. But by slow down I mean I want to transfer the responsibilities, because I know my sons are more capable, the two of them together, than myself. They can keep up with the changing times. I know that; common sense tells me that I have to do that. They can't believe that I'm as active as I can be. In fact my children say, I can still outrun them even at my age of 77. There's no substitute for experience, I know that. What's interesting in the wine business is we are just getting started. I've been saying that for the last fifty years. They now all know we are just getting started because there's so much more research that we have to do, both in viticultural practice and winemaking. They are all convinced of that now, so it's quite a challenge and I'm very happy that I'm able to turn that over to them.

Even as a youngster I always wanted to excel in whatever I was doing. I knew my mother could excel in cooking and I had great admiration for my father, in terms as to what he did in business. Maybe I wanted to mimic him in that way. They were both an inspiration as I was growing up. When I went into the wine business I wanted to find out if could I excel, and what I could do. Once I found that I could do something in the business then I went forward and I stopped at nothing to attain it.

My parents were very supportive, very open and loving. They instilled confidence in me. They allowed me and my brother to do whatever we wanted, and in turn we would do anything for them. We had about $15,000 dollars in the bank for our school education and we lent that to my father during the Depression, when things were tough. He promised to send us to whatever school we wanted to go to and he kept his promise.

I am alot like my father. He was a man of his word. I have always had a real affection for him. He was a man of very few words, a shrug of a shoulder or a look is all he needed to communicate his feelings.

Basically speaking we worked; we learned to work. My parents were Italian immigrants when they came here. We believed in them strongly and we wanted to satisfy them, we looked at them as our mentors and role models. My mother was a terrific cook and a terrific mother. I didn't know how good she was until we had the three-star chefs of France over here. Then I realized how good my mother was.

One day my father came to me when I was a junior at Stanford. My brother was there too, but a year behind me. My father wanted to know what we were going to do after graduating from college. I said I was interested in the business world, and he then told me that he thought there was a future in the wine business. That was in 1935, more than a year after repeal of prohibition, and I figured why not start with a young business and grow with it. My father told me that Napa Valley was the outstanding wine growing region for both red and white table wine. In my senior year I took chemistry and was tutored by a professor who taught enology at the University of California in Berkeley. I subsequently went to work for my father. It was a very important decision for me.

When we were doing business with the Bank of America, I went to my local banker to ask for credit. The banker said, "OK, fine." Well the next thing I knew, the local banker reneged on his word. Mr. Ferrogero, chairman of the Finance Committee of the Bank of America, put us in what we call "warehousing". When we were placed into warehousing it meant that we had to work through another party to release our wine. That was a blow to our integrity; I was really broken up about that. I vowed that I was going to get us out of that situation. That experience really solidified the family.

Then, of course, there was the big blowup when I was released and put on a leave of absence from Charles Krug, which was six years after the death of my father. When my father passed away, there was an honest difference of opinion on what should be done with the business. Because of my enthusiasm and my outgoingness, Fred Ferrogero, a business advisor to my mother, felt that my brother was best suited to direct the business. My brother didn't want to move as fast as I was moving. I must have given the impression at that time that I was a dreamer and impractical in my ideas.

My personal and business philosophy has always been to deal with people with complete integrity, openness, and honesty. I've always felt that I am a realist. I like to face the facts whatever they are, that the one thing that's unique about me. There are many people who go around the bush about things, and they're not straight forward. I don't want to do business that way. I have always wanted to be open, honest, and above board. I am willing to put total involvement, total dedication into what I do. My word is my bond just like my father.

I have always had real confidence. I knew that there was alot that I would have to learn in life and I was willing to put the time and effort into doing it. I think maybe that's one of my attributes. If I really worked at something and I believed in it, it would come true. My instincts have never let me down. I've been very fortunate.

I was brought up as a strict Catholic. I had Dominican sisters that taught me in a very strict and impeccable way. If I did not accomplish something the way the sisters wanted it, I developed a feeling of guilt and inadequacy. I became a perfectionist in everything that I did. From that early experience I have always had this feeling that I was inadequate. Well now I find that human beings aren't perfect, and I am far from it.

I'm becoming much more realistic in what I'm doing now and I have more peace of mind. I've accomplished things that people said I could not accomplish. I thought we could produce wine belonging in the same company of the world's finest and we did it. I always felt that I wanted to raise the image of our country. I knew we had the natural resources. I knew we had the climate, the soil, and the grapes, and we were developing the knowledge and the know-how to be the best.

This is what I'll be able to pass over to the younger generation and to my children. This gives me great satisfaction, to perfect our process, but it also raises the image of our country in the eyes of the world. Culturally speaking, the world thinks of us in terms of hamburgers and hotdogs, that we are not as cultured in wine and food. Well, that attitude is beginning to change.

I think that you have to feel satisfied within yourself with whatever you do in life. If you want to excel in anything you have to be totally involved and totally committed. You also have to look at the good things of life. You know, we are an imperfect lot, we human beings. If you look at the good side of people, realizing that everyone has shortcomings, you will be a much happier, more accepting person. That's very important, because if you're unhappy you can never really excel. Take stock at what you're doing and then set a goal for yourself, not beyond what you can reach, but set a realistic goal. We have to allow for flexibility in ourselves and others.

Always look back where you came from; it's a humbling experience. Sometimes if we move too quickly we forget where we came from. You need to have a proper perspective of what you're doing in life. When I think about myself, the qualities I feel that I have and have done well for me are integrity, honesty, enthusiasm, and the good Lord has given me a lot of energy along with that.

PART TWO

Staying Active

Melvin Belli

CHAPTER SEVEN

Melvin Belli

Trial attorney Melvin M. Belli, Sr. heads a California law firm with branch offices in San Francisco, Los Angeles, Sacramento, San Diego, and Carmel. Mr. Belli is in his law offices everyday, remains involved in news-making and precedent setting legal cases, continues to write books, and frequently does pro bono legal and community work.

Born July 29, 1907 in Sonora, California, Belli's forbearers were early California bankers and educators. After graduating from the University of California-Boalt School of Law in 1933, Belli assumed the role of an indigent as a part of service with the Federal Government. Traveling by boxcar, he wrote a report on the Depression's effects on the vagrant population of the United States. His report was used as the basis for transient-relief programs throughout the nation.

Among Belli's well-known cases are defense of Jack Ruby, Mae West, Errol Flynn, Tony Curtis, Lenny Bruce, Martha Mitchell, Lana Turner, The Rolling Stones, and Muhammed Ali. Belli has also represented many clients involved in mass tragedies over the years: the MGM Grand Hotel fire in Las Vegas, the collapse of the Kansas City Hyatt Walkway, the Korean Jet Liner disaster, the Bendectin birth defect cases, and the Bhopal/Union Carbide isocyanate gas disaster. Belli has been the president of many professional organizations. He has also written 62 legal publications as popularized works. He was once justifiably referred to in Life *Magazine as "The King of Torts".*

—◆—

Portraits of Passion: Aging, Defying the Myth

I think that my main purpose in life is doing what comes naturally. I just wanted to be where the action was, and that's the reason, I guess, that I became a lawyer. Law holds it all together and if it weren't for lawyers and judges, particularly the good ones, this wouldn't be the greatest country in the world. I think we have a great way for making this the greatest country. We do what we want within limits: such as freedom of movement, speech, and of thought.

So I keep on working, because this is where the action is, and that's what I've wanted and that's what I got and that's what I'll continue to do. If I stop working I think that I would just vegetate. I can't conceive how a fellow says, I'm going to retire, and I'm not going to work, or I'm going to take up yachting, or I'm going to travel. Any of those things don't substitute for being where the action is, particularly when you're part of the action. That's why I'm a trial lawyer, because people make the world. They're the one's who make the laws. They're the ones who make the things go. They do everything but bring the moon and the stars out. So I'm very, very happy with what I'm doing and I wouldn't want to do anything else.

I get my travel from my cases, because I've tried cases all over the world. When I travel it's a lot more fun going to a place knowing that I'll be working in my profession. To go to Paris just to see the sights is not for me. I want to be part of the sights, part of the core. That's why when I go to a foreign country, I head for the courts the first thing, to see the barristers and judges, and then I'll spend time in their libraries. Indeed I once wrote a pamphlet at Lincoln's Inn in London.

Looking back on my childhood I'd say my family gave me security and comfort. It was a very secure thing, a very loving thing, and a very close family with aunts, uncles, cousins and grandparents, no brothers or sisters unfortunately. We'd go over to the homes of various grandmothers, grandfathers, and people in the family for every holiday. We were just a loving, close typical American family, enjoying the American holidays, the American way of life.

I've often thought how I would have turned out, if I were brought up in the Bronx, or someplace else. Would I have turned out to be a better man? It's a hard question to answer. I do not know how I would have met the challenges of a less secure childhood, or got caught up in drugs or crime, or juvenile delinquency. I do not know if I would have had the strength of character to have resisted the temptations. I think so, but I also think I would have been better off had I had more challenge and more discomfort, more insecurity as a child.

When I look back on what a beautiful secure childhood I had: of the holiday festivities, dinners with the family gathered around, the big house with the warm, huge fireplace and everybody dressed in their holiday finest with snow outside, firecrackers on the fourth of July, it is heartwarming.

There was always challenge in school. I just wanted to be where the action was. If there was a race I wanted to be in it. If there was a race I wanted to see the pits where the cars were.

I was very curious and very inquisitive as a child. I would read everything I could get my hands on. I think one of my great crutches in my upbringing was the *Book of Knowledge*. That had a great index, and if you know how to use indexes you can find anything in the law. That's where I got my start.

Teachers, clergy people, and the people that were in contact with my family had a great influence on me. I think that was part of my father being the village banker. I was expected to be out in front. I was challenging, I was reading, I was inquisitive, and I wanted to see beyond the horizon all the time -- well beyond.

My mother was the daughter of the town druggist. My grandmother was the first woman druggist in California! She was a character of characters. Everybody knew her far and wide, the indians, everybody else. I was the heir to all of that.

I remember when my grandmother died, what a terrible tragedy that was because she was the matriarch of the whole family. She loved me and I loved her very much. Her dying and the loss of my first dog were really devastating to me. Later on when I was in college, when my dad lost all his money, I found that didn't bother or depress me very much. I have never been very much concerned with money. I'm more concerned I think when others lose it. I had will power to just move on and continue on with my life.

Now I pray more and talk to my own personal God. There must be a supreme being who put this whole thing together, or partly together. We are limited. We don't have the computers in our brain. We don't even have the words or the thoughts to contemplate what is the beginning and what is end. We can't conceive of it. We haven't the capacity to conceive it. I know the beginning of philosophy starts with "cognito ergo sum", (I know therefore I am), but that doesn't satisfy me, that doesn't explain reality. The fact that I'm asking questions about it shouldn't be the answer.

I've recently heard behind my back, "He's 82, he's over the hill." I know that isn't the fact, because I'm sharper now than I ever have been. I do have some failing and fading for current memory. In some instances someone will give me a name and I can't remember it 5 minutes later, but it pops back after a period of time. My memory for things that happened in the past is much better than it ever has been. That's the reason that I like to argue cases and stand in front of a jury, because when I stand up there the stuff all comes back in a warm historical reminiscence.

I think I'm sharper than I've ever been. It has convinced me to look for an older doctor, because he's not only got the experience, he's probably run across whatever the pathology is before and knows how to handle it. As science has improved, he's exposed to the latest advance in medicine along with his own personal experience. I think that an older doctor, an older lawyer has more pleasure, more fun, and is better equipped to serve you, his client or his patient, providing that he isn't one of the unfortunates that ages young. There are a lot of people that I've seen that should leave the bench in their 50's and 60's. Conversely they're a lot of them that not only should stay on, but should look forward to being older and becoming even more brilliant.

I'm enjoying life now just as much. I look better now than I have in years (I lost 75 pounds). I'm thinking better and faster, better cerebration I think, than ever before. I'm not quite as active as I used to be. The hedonistic things have been cut down.

It's called willpower, and I don't think that that is an inclusive term. I think that the best example is cutting down on the things that you like to eat. I had to do that. I don't believe that we know all of the answers on diet, but I think that I have an innate feeling on what I should or shouldn't be eating. So really, I haven't any complaints.

I think that the best time of day for me is when I go to my big bed at night. I think about things I could have done that day and things I am going to do the next day. Also the intangible things, like saying hello to people, being friendly with people. I think these outward manifestations make you better off inside, and make you a better person. Reaching out and being friendly, I think that's one of the main things in life.

You've got to love what you're doing. If you're fortunate, you've chosen your profession and had the incentive to go into that particular profession at the very beginning of your career. Does it fulfill all your drive? Is it where people are, where the action is, where you're the leader, where you're helping people? You're not only making material gains for yourself personally, but you're helping people while you're doing it. You have the best of both worlds there, doing for others and doing for yourself. I think that's a principal thing.

I've said if you go into the profession that you want to go into, if you continue to like it, then you've got to help it grow and help yourself grow. You wouldn't help your profession to grow if you didn't like it, if it didn't come naturally to you. The feeling of charity and giving to your fellow man is an important ingredient. We do a lot of pro bono stuff that we don't get any fee on. We have lots of that. In law, you're doing something for somebody else. That's why it's such a great profession, like being a doctor.

I'll work as long as I can, just like I'm doing it now, continue to go to trial the same way that I've always done. And while trial law may be principally an intellectual and vigorous battle, I do believe that it's more important than ever to be reminded "Forgive us our trespasses as we forgive those who trespass against us."

Moon H. Yuen

CHAPTER EIGHT

Moon H. Yuen

Moon Yuen was born in China and came to the United States in 1939. In 1942, he went into the American military and fought in Europe. He was wounded and later discharged in 1946. He received a B.S. in Electrical Engineering from Healds Engineering College in 1948, a Business Administration Certificate from the University of California Extension in 1970, and an Engineering Ph.D. from Pacific Western University in 1986.

He worked for the Bechtel Corporation for 27 years and eventually started his own company in 1975. He is a member of the Institute of Electrical and Electronic Engineers, Chinese-American Institute of Engineers and Scientists, the National Council of Engineering Examiners, and Asian-American Architects and Engineers.

Moon Yuen has received many civic awards including the Distinguished Community Services Award from the San Francisco Board of Supervisors in 1987, the Distinguished Achievement in Engineering Award from the AAAE in both 1985 and 1989, and was the first Bechtel employee in seventy years to receive the Teacher of the Year Award from their Technical Development Program. He is a prolific writer and researcher, having published 30 technical articles, papers, publications, and patents. In addition to his professional commitments, Moon has found time since 1984 to work as co-Chairperson for the Annual Fund Raising Committee of Self-Help for the Elderly of San Francisco. He is the embodiment of hard work and positive thinking.

❖

Portraits of Passion: Aging, Defying the Myth

I continue to work for personal satisfaction. I believe age should not limit a person's accomplishments. I believe working is healthy for everyone. I feel I contribute through my work.

One of my golden rules is giving. When I am with a group of scientists and engineers, I would say to them, "you give to get more." They think that I am abnormal. In a scientific formula you never get more than you put in. Like an electrical motor, you put a thousand watts of power in, you get about 850 watts of work out, but with people you get more than you give.

If I quit working for my company, I will still have enough to get by. Personally I don't need the income for myself. I could live simply. My wife and I are both very simple people. But with this extra money I earn I can do the things that I want to do. I have many projects, not only in the United States, but in other countries: for example, an orphanage in Taiwan. I've been working with them for 17 years. I have also been sponsoring children for the past few years through the *Children International.* I can use money to do a lot of good, realizing that people need both your money and your time.

I was born in a village in the province of Canton in Southern China. My mother was probably one of the kindest women in the world, very loving, poor yet sacrificing to take care of her children. I recall the Depression of the 1930's, in the United States and the rest of the world. My father was in Canada as a laborer. For those years, he didn't send any money home. We had a piece of land in the village. My mother, my sister, and myself, we all worked the farm to survive. I remember almost every day there were beggars come to our house for food, just to survive. My mother always shared whatever was left, a bowl of rice, or gave them whatever we had.

I attended elementary school in the village. A Buddhist temple was used as our schoolhouse. We had a teacher who refused to give up teaching Confucian philosophy. I remember a great number of kids who left our school and attended schools in other villages to learn newer things, but I somehow stuck with him and learned about the teachings of Confucius. I still adhere to this philosophy today. After I came to America, Sister Mary in the Catholic High School near San Francisco's Chinatown gave me my first job as a substitute janitor. I didn't even know how to mop floors. I never touched a broom when I was in China. Sister Mary would always say, "Be proud of what you're doing. A janitor is as important as a teacher or anybody else. But what is important is that you must do a good job. Do it so you're proud of it." She gave me a letter of recommendation when I needed it to find my school job. She was my first mentor in the United States. It's encouraging to know somebody cares for you.

When I look at my life I feel good about my past. Although I did some struggling. Prejudice was very strong against the Chinese at the time I came here. I had experienced a lot of racial prejudice. That is why I have been a board member of Chinese for Affirmative Action since 1982. One of CAA's objectives is to fight racial prejudice. Many immigrants came to the United States the same time I did in 1939. A lot of young people went to work right away. I was one of the few who decided to continue their education. In school I was treated like an outcast by other students.

My oldest son got in trouble when he was young. Being the first son, when something like that happens in a Chinese family, it is very disgraceful in my culture. I reached out to him and got him help. My relationship to my son is very important to me, it has been very painful. I got through it, and it made me more humble and a more understanding person. Perhaps there may be millions of people who need help and are less fortunate. Where there is a family in need if I think I can help, I will. I belong to the YMCA, which helps the young people. I always try to play an important part in the fund raising for the annual scholarships sponsored by the Chinese American Institute of Engineers and Scientists. I go to Taiwan two or three times a year to plan for various self-help programs. This is one of my secrets, when you're so busy doing things, you don't have time to think about your problems.

I believe in the teachings of Confucius, of Taoism, and of Jesus Christ. If you get down to the basics, there's not much difference. It's all universal, they all teach us to live a good and full life. However. I often wonder why that in the Chinese teaching of Confucius or Taoism it is said that the child was born perfect, no sin, absolutely beautiful. Jesus teaches that you are a sinner when you are born. It took me a long time to reconcile this difference. For many years I refused to be a Christian because of the conflict. But after a great deal of soul searching, I became more peaceful about this inner conflict. I overcame my resistance as I learned more and more about Christianity.

In my opinion, one must follow some sort of a guideline of what you believe in. A lot of people who call themselves Christians, they do not practice what they preach. They don't live by the Golden Rule. I

Portraits of Passion: Aging, Defying the Myth

was so shocked when I came here as a young man and learned about the high divorce rate in the United States. In my old country, China, we don't know about divorce. In the village I lived in through my childhood, we never locked the door when we went to bed. People never took your belongings.

I really never pay much attention to how old I am. Basically I'm very healthy at 68 plus. My weight and blood pressure are good. I exercise regularly. I am a disciplined person, I work on my own schedule. I eat carefully and simply, and I take care of my body. I think when a person has a healthy body his mind is directed toward healthy things. Fortunately, in the Chinese community, age is respected. Even now, you go to any setting of dinner, a marriage, or a social activity, people respect age for whatever we have done. We hold on to that tradition which I feel is an important value for the younger generation.

I have a long-term goal. I want to live to at least the year 2005, for two reasons. I want to be here for the 21st Century. To do that I've got to keep healthy. And I have several projects that will probably take more than 10 years to accomplish: the orphanage in Taiwan, a project to start computer training for the students when they get out of high school. We need money to buy computers. Being an orphanage, it's privately funded which required fund raising. I also have a long-term project in my village. We never had a good schoolhouse in the village. So my wife and I have to give time and money to complete the school building program. This will make my childhood dream come true...some day I will build a school for my village.

I think the little talent I have is that I'm a person that's easy to get along with. I love people. I don't care who they are. I will always give. I believe that everybody must have something good in him. In the philosophy of giving, I believe to this day, you always get more than you give.

Alice Yarish

CHAPTER NINE

Alice Yarish

Alice Yarish was born on April 25, 1909 in Goldfield, Nevada. She received her B.A. degree in English from the University of Southern California, and did graduate work in Law at Southwestern University. She has 30 years experience as an investigative reporter, editor, and columnist on a number of newspapers including the Marin Independent Journal, Santa Rosa Press Democrat, *the* Novato Advance, San Francisco Examiner, *and has written for the* Pacific Sun *for eight years.*

Some of her honors include: First prize, San Francisco Press Club in 1973 for her reporting of corruption in the Marin County Drug Abuse Bureau, and second prize in 1974 for her investigation of the plight of single mothers; Third prize, Associated Press Writing Competition; Distinguished Coverage Award, Marin Mental Health Association.

In 1990 Mrs. Yarish was elected to the Marin County Women's Hall of Fame for her journalism and civic activities.

Mrs. Yarish has just completed an autobiographical manuscript entitled, Growing Old Disgracefully-Adventures of a Maverick Journalist. *She is still an active writer and freelance journalist. She has 4 grown children and 7 grandchildren.*

———❖———

My mother and father were both lawyers. My mother had been a journalist before she became a lawyer. She became the first woman to practice law in the State of Nevada in 1906. My father was a judge and a lawyer, and he was particularly interested in politics. He used to encourage me to take an interest in civic affairs and what society needed to improve life in general and the status of the individual. My dad and I read together from the time I was two until he died when I was 26. He was an extremely well-read man. When I learned to read, we started out with Peter Rabbit and then we went on up through Mark Twain, the Oz books, Robert Louis Stevenson, Dickens, Thackeray and Shakespeare. When I got to college I was a very literate person. I'm sure that I learned writing through this prolific reading program we had.

My father was a versatile man, and he enjoyed life. He was very witty, charming, and had lots of friends. He was a great bridge player. But when my mother died, he just kind of fell apart.

My parents never wanted me to be just the ordinary female worker like teacher, nurse, clerk. They both wanted me to venture out. I went to law school for two years, planning to work with my father, but Dad closed his office, and I had to quit school because he died shortly afterward and I had to go to work. I might have become a lawyer as my brother and five nephews did. My parents were very bright, very well informed. They were very helpful to me when I was growing up.

I think one of the persons that had the greatest influence on me was Dr. Roswell Johnson, who was co-director of the first family-relations advisory agency, the American Institute of Family Relations. When I was a social worker dealing with broken families, Dr. Johnson taught me the elements of temperament and personality that were constructive, and those that were destructive. I felt he had a great deal of influence on my subsequent attitudes and behavior in life.

I got my first full-time job as a journalist on a daily newspaper when I was 43 and had four little kids. I always loved newspapers. So when I got a full-time job on a newspaper, my life just turned around. I got really happy. I loved the work, I got better jobs, better assignments all the time. I won a number of awards and gained a good deal of recognition. It was very rewarding to me. As an investigative reporter I turned up a lot of stuff on the Narcotics Bureau that the other papers didn't mention. I did all kinds of others things, too. On the *Pacific Sun* I had a great deal of personal freedom to write about whatever I wanted to write, and in unconventional style.

I worked until I was 73, but I had accomplished something for which I've advocated a long time. I went to part-time retirement instead of full retirement. I had two part-time jobs, one on the *Pacific Sun*, one on the *San Francisco Examiner.* I retired from the *Sun* when I was 68 and then I kept a half-time job until I was 73. I've long been an advocate of part-time retirement for people, so that they don't have to quit all at once "cold turkey". I think part-time work is important for all working people, because of the dreadful change that takes place when they stop work and go suddenly into retirement. They don't know what to do with their time. So they go out looking for part-time jobs, which are very hard to get. But if they could retire just half-time, or say they would cut down one day a week for four years, they could adjust to retirement gradually.

The unspoken message is that retirement leaves some people feeling lost and bored. Half-retirement means you have something to do. You're using your expertise. You're still earning some money. You are perhaps acting as a training officer for the people that replace you in a job. It's easier on management, because they replace you at a lower wage scale in part-time and it's good for the retirement fund because it only takes a portion of your retirement pay. So everybody benefits.

Without a doubt my last 20 years have been my best years. and my 80th year the best year of all. It's because I had gotten free of the things that had made me unhappy. I ran away from home when I was 59 and left my husband.

I had three bad experiences in life. My teenage years were very unhappy. The deadly Depression was terrible, and my marriage was unhappy.

The Depression had a terrible influence on me. I walked the streets for three years looking for a job after I graduated from college. I wanted to get into newspaper work, but I couldn't because they were laying people off instead of hiring. So I joined the only profession that flourishes in hard times, that of a social welfare worker. It was so discouraging, as a social worker I was working with the poverty-stricken people. I can relate to the homeless today. I think homelessness is dreadful. And I say, "there but for the grace of God go I."

My present goal is to get my book published. I think my ability as a writer was the thing that I'm proudest of, had the most success with, and enjoyed the most. I'm a good writer. People think of me as jolly, fun, and amusing, and that I like. All my friends are much younger than I. I don't have any friends in my age group. I would say that my daughter-in-law, who's about 40, is my very best friend. Today I'm at my best, I couldn't be better off than I am right now, very happy. I try to have a good time everyday. I have lots of friends, wonderful children and grandchildren, and I love my home.

I think that it's very important to enjoy life. You have to start that when you're young. You have to learn to appreciate the good things in life and to enjoy what's going on. I enjoy sports. I like the arts, opera, music. I read an awful lot. I think some people age well because they have a rich life. One thing I discovered when I was a social worker, working with the aged during the Depression, that the older people who had hobbies, interests, who had extracurricular activities adjusted to old age much better than people who had not developed interests and hobbies and extra-vocational activities. Those people had something to fall back on when they were no longer employable. They were much better adjusted and happier. If you have those interests when you're younger they'll carry on and sustain you.

Alice Faye

CHAPTER TEN

Alice Faye

Born in New York City's Hell's Kitchen in 1915, Alice Jean Leppert began her theatrical career at 14, as a dancer. At age 17, Alice was discovered by legendary singer and film star Rudy Vallee. In 1934, she was asked to replace the female lead in the film version of George White's Scandals. *With the release of the film she was offered a contract with Twentieth Century-Fox.*

Alice Faye co-starred with many of Hollywood's most dashing leading men, including Tyrone Power, Spencer Tracy, and Dick Powell. Among Alice's considerable cinematic achievements are such notable films as: On the Avenue *(1937),* You Can't Have Everything *(1937),* In Old Chicago *(1938),* Rose of Washington Square *(1939), and* Lillian Russell *(1940). Alice retired from films in 1945 to be with her husband, entertainer Phil Harris, and her two young daughters. In 1962, she returned to the screen to star with Pat Boone and Ann-Margret in* State Fair.

For the past six years, Alice has been "Ambassador to Good Health" to older Americans for Pfizer Pharmaceutical Company. She has written a book called Growing Older, Staying Young. *Today she is a grandmother and keeps very active living what she preaches about good health.*[13]

---- ❖ ----

I try to practice what I preach, and that is that staying active and involved is very important to people that are aging.

You can't sit around and do nothing. I'm very fortunate that I have a job at this stage of the game. I'm able to stay active and involved.

Portraits of Passion: Aging, Defying the Myth

That's what it's all about. I've always been aware of being productive. I liked to swim at the YWCA in New York, I always ice skated and danced. I was always active, it's part of my nature.

My exercise routine began when I was forty, I went to Elizabeth Arden's Main Chance in Phoenix, Arizona. I'd never been any place like that before. I never felt better than when I was there exercising, swimming, and watching intake of sugar and fats. When I was working in films I had no routine. I just worked and believe me, when you made films you didn't have to exercise. You got plenty of it on the sound stages doing those musicals, singing and dancing at the studios all day and dancing at the night clubs by night. Now walking and swimming are my favorite forms of exercise. Walking is probably the greatest form of exercise for most people.

When I was young I didn't have time to go to the movies. I was working all the time, that was my background. I came from New York City. I came from the West Side of New York City. My mother worked. My father worked. My grandmother raised me. I went to school, I ice skated after school, and did those sort of things.

I keep my sanity by working, by staying busy. It makes me happy to be able to go out and see fans. It's a personal thing. I kind of relate to being part of their families, some of them, not all of them. It makes me happy. They're young elders. They're people my age. They remember me. They relate to me in their family. It's a wonderful thing. It's a great privilege to be able to do what I do. I get a kick out of doing it and I'm thankful to God I can do it.

I'm just a working person. I just like to work, it's been my whole life. I'm just a normal person. I've been in show business all of my life. When your in show business, you take care of yourself. You want to look good because you're standing in front of thousands of people. Some people are maybe kind of lazy. They sit in the rocker and don't want to get up. It's never too late! Never! Once they get started they will never want to stop.

I don't look back, I look ahead. I just want to feel good and I want to stay active and involved and enjoy life. That's about it. I'm not making a big thing out of it.

I pattern my life after what I call, "The Pfizer Five": stay active and involved, eat a well-balanced diet, don't smoke, exercise two to three times a week see your doctor whenever necessary and follow his or her instructions to the letter. And I add a sixth point; for heavens sake, have a sense of humor. I'm going on my seventh year working for Pfizer. I go out three days every month. We fly all over the nation. I travelled over 100,000 miles to address state conferences on aging, to meet with governors and make personal appearances at senior expos, fitness walks and community groups. It's wonderful!

Herb Rosen

CHAPTER ELEVEN

Herb Rosen

Herb Rosen was born in New York on September 1, 1922.
He received his BS Degree from the College of the City of New
York in 1943, and subsequently received his MSW from the
Columbia University School of Social Work in 1945. He
became a social worker, caseworker and supervisor in
residential treatment centers for emotionally disturbed
children.

Mr. Rosen was supervisor for child welfare in the city of
San Francisco for 13 years. He later transferred to the
trauma unit of San Francisco General Hospital, and is now
an on call social worker at Mt. Zion Hospital in San
Francisco. He is married with two children and four
grandchildren.

———— ❖ ————

I feel very fortunate at this time in my life. I am what is known as an 'on call' social worker substitute, working for social workers who are absent for whatever reason. This schedule leaves time for play. I feel that after working full-time for forty years, I'd like to pursue other things that interest me. That's what time is about to me. I play tennis three or four times a week, and I swim almost every day. I feel that this activity has kept me well physically. For the last twenty-five years I've maintained the same weight by watching my diet carefully .

The concern about my health comes from an adverse experience in my life at the age of twenty-nine. I was suddenly struck down with tuberculosis. I had to go to a sanitarium for a year and a half. I had surgery which collapsed one-half of my right lung. Like the characters in Thomas Mann's, *Magic Mountain*, I had a year and a half to contemplate my life and felt very determined to live life as full and as healthful as I can. The good news was I recovered. I'm very well, and the great thing is I stopped smoking at that particular time.

I didn't go as far as Norman Cousins in his use of humor to recover from disease, but I agree with him in the sense that I found it very important as a defense against the vicissitudes of life. Humor has always played a role in my life. I'll give you an example. When I was at the tuberculosis sanitarium, we had a little patient newspaper, a mimeographed job, and I had a column that was called "No Bed of Rosen". I indulged in the black humor that you find in sanitariums. I used it with patients I work with in the hospitals I was assigned to, also. I have found that most patients respond to humor as a way of lightening their psychological load. People who are patients in hospitals are vulnerable. They are naked unto the Lord, helpless, they just lie there. I found that most people want to laugh, wherever they are. It's a great buffer against the hard facts of their reality. I enjoyed making people laugh, not only patients in the hospital, but in general. I've used humor throughout my life. I guess I am a frustrated comedian. My father was a printing pressman. He was a very funny guy. The one thing that my brother and I got from him, is our sense of humor.

I have felt for a long time that my older brother played a large part in helping to develop my intellect. As a youngster I tried to emulate him as best I could. He was always a very fine guy, and I think that my sense of justice and feelings for human beings comes from him. My mother was a very religious person. We did get from her the Yiddish virtue of charity. I think that Judaism as a philosophy, the moral aspects, the emphasis on education, on justice and family, was a very important foundation for my code of ethics. Of all the subjects I've read and researched, the whole Jewish history has impressed me. How this group has survived the horrors that have been thrust upon them astounds me. It's been a great source of inspiration for me. Both of our parents instilled in us the curiosity about life through learning. Education was greatly stressed as the way for children of immigrants to better their lives.

Being married to my wife, Maggie, all these years has been wonderful. She is a very fine woman and an accomplished artist. We both love to travel. We have visited many different countries, and made many wonderful friends abroad. I find that there aren't enough days, or enough hours in the day for me to pursue all my activities. One of our great joys is spending time with our grandchildren who live in Halifax, Nova Scotia, and on the Russian River.

I basically sing my song from day to day, enjoying the things I do. I have a reputation as a great communicator, because I like to fashion relationships. I feel people should like to get together. I like to see people happy. I'm a giver and I'm also a taker. I take from relationships. I take from my job with patients and use that experience to help me with others. At my age I feel life is all very precious. I want to live as much as I can while I'm well, and do all I can.

I've never faced age discrimination as I have heard others talk about it. In fact, the opposite occurs. People think I am a lot younger than I really am. We age slowly in my family. My mother is 101 years old and she still has dark eyebrows. I've got a white beard and white payas (sideburns), my hair is still brown, so people think that I'm much younger than I really am.

When I look back now, life is much easier. As a Depression kid a penny was a lot of money, and I used to walk two miles to college to save a nickel. Fortunately my wife and I can live comfortably, and that's very important. Because being older in today's world without financial stability can be devastating physically and emotionally.

As an older person you have a right to do something or do nothing. You can just hang out if you want to. The main thing is to find things you like to do. If you don't have activities that you can do yourself, be a volunteer in some community agency. You can get a lot of satisfaction out of doing that. There are a lot of people out there that can use your help. You have to find the right balance of activity and personal fulfillment. Unfortunately there's an emphasis on telling people who retire, you better have a program, you'd better have something scheduled every moment otherwise you'll go crazy. Because, you've been going to work all your life, living a structured existence.

There are two things in terms of the future that I'd like to be around for awhile to see. I'd love to see my four grandchildren become adults. I love them dearly, and I have a wonderful relationship with them. It's like a novel that hasn't been written yet. I can't wait for it to go on, and for me to be involved with them as long as I possibly can. I am also fascinated by the way the world is turning and evolving. The things that are happening now that I had never dreamed of could occur for humankind. So it's a curiosity or a desire to be around as long as I can to see the grandchildren become established adults, and to see the world progress to a point where things will be better for all people.

Well at this point, I'd like to quote my very close friend Bernie Saperstein, the great Jewish Philosopher of West 89th Street in New York. His advice is, "stay healthy, every thing else is whipped cream."

John W. Gardner

CHAPTER TWELVE

John W. Gardner

John Gardner was born in Los Angeles in 1912. He attended Stanford University where he received his A.B. degree "with great distinction," and later his M.A. degree in Psychology. During his undergraduate years he set a number of Pacific Coast Inter-Collegiate records in swimming, and holds the Distinguished Achievement Medal of the Stanford Athletic Board. He received his Ph.D. from the University of California in 1938.

Doctor Gardner was the editor of President Kennedy's book To Turn The Tide, *and is the author of the books* Excellence, Self-Renewal, No Easy Victories, The Recovery of Confidence, In Common Cause, *and* Morale. *He is the co-editor, with Francesca Gardner Reese, of* Quotations of Wit and Wisdom (Know or Listen to Those Who Know). *His new book,* On Leadership, *was published in 1990.*

Gardner served as Secretary of HEW from 1965 to 1968. He was Chairman of President Johnson's Task Force on Education, and of the White House Conference on Education (1965). He was a member of President Carter's Commission on an Agenda for the Eighties. During 1981-82 he served as a member of President Reagan's Task Force on Private Sector Initiatives.

In 1964, Mr. Gardner was awarded the Presidential Medal of Freedom. Among other awards he has received are the AFL-CIO Murray-Green Award, the United Auto Workers' Social Justice Award, the U.S. Air Force Exceptional Services Award, and the Public Welfare Medal of the National Academy of Science.

❖

Portraits of Passion: Aging, Defying the Myth

My whole family is a high-energy family that likes to keep moving. A more important factor in my own case is that I've always believed the meaning of life stems from committing yourself to significant goals. I don't think those goals disappear when you're sixty-five.

My mother was the main influence in my life, because my father died when I was a year old. My mother instilled in both my brother and myself a fairly strong feeling that we should be busy on "serious" work, so to speak. But beyond that, if my life experience is my guide, that is what keeps the sense of meaning in life, that's what gives you the strength to endure the things you have to endure. You have goals, you have purposes, and you continue.

I've spent some time thinking about what the goals are for me. The interesting thing is that they change through the years, particularly if you review them periodically. If you don't give the matter any thought, then life becomes a kind of an escalator, you just ride up. Your jobs tend to set your goals, and you discover that you've let that happen without asking yourself, "What should I be doing? What are goals for me?"

So you really have to take a close look inward in terms of your experience and your longevity, to discover what you feel is important to pursue. My own feeling is that you should be doing that all of your life, so when you get to be sixty-five it becomes a matter of necessity: no crutches. You're faced with a blank calendar unless you say to yourself, "Here's what I'm going to set as goals." I think that for most people diversion is monotony and leisure is monotony. The human organism is designed for action, designed for goal seeking and problem-solving.

I had good teachers and when I went into psychology I had excellent professors, some of whom I wanted to emulate. But I didn't really find the kind of mentoring that tends to shape your life until I was in my thirties. Then I did encounter some people holding highly responsible jobs, but also with keen feelings for their cities, their country, and their community.

One was Devereux Josephs, who was the president of Carnegie Corporation when I was hired. He had a big impact on me as an individual who was accustomed to thinking and acting responsibly on a broader scale than I was used to. I was responsible but narrow. I'd always been a professional or a Marine, I hadn't thought that much about the way the country ran or the world ran. So working with him was influential.

I came back from the War with a new attitude. When I was in Italy in Marine Corps uniform, I began to think about the fact that my life had been totally disrupted twice: once with the Great Depression, once with the War. And I had never once seriously addressed myself to how the world functioned or how the country functioned. What produced these great events that disrupted my life?

I first wanted to be a writer, which is by nature a rather solitary thing. Then I went into psychology, and I was very much an academic psychologist. My teaching, my writing, my research in the field of psychology were rather narrowly conceived. So, to come out into the world was a big change for me. I concluded in Italy that I had better take a broader view of what the world was doing and how it functioned.

I am now teaching a course in a graduate school of business course.

Just the other day I emphasized to the class that they must never underestimate the sources of energy that exist within them, that will be tapped if they find things that stir them. If they pursue their deepest interests, it will pull them into action.

You have to tap your own motivations, your deepest motivations. I've done that for a lot of years and I find it extremely rewarding. I took the same approach when I was sixty-four and stepping down from Common Cause. I told my mother, who at the time was about eighty-six, "I'm not sure what I'm going to do next year," and she said, "Next year?! Johnny, you need a twenty-year plan!" She was right!

Until you go down physically, you can be vital, dynamic in your way of thinking and approaching life. And in fact, it will postpone the moment of physical decay.

I think early events led me to the conviction that I'd better be in charge of my life. We moved a lot and I was in a great many strange schools. I came out of that more independent of the group than are most young people.

I would describe my upbringing as very much influenced by the Protestant Ethic--do the right thing, work hard. I have a strong streak of religious motivation in me, which has led me to explore a lot of religions and to become very much at home in some. I feel totally at home in the whole Judeo-Christian ethic.

As you get older, people see you as an older person, and are less inclined to put you on committees, less inclined to see you as an active participant. My whole temperament is such that I do not accept the possibility. I just don't. I don't accept it and I don't allow such feelings in myself.

Obviously decline occurs.I think anyone's who's seventy-seven would be lying if they told you that they have never wondered about the rate of decline. I mean, it's real. It's real in your sixties, even in your fifties.

But it isn't a unitary thing. I can't run as fast as I could in my forties, but I have improved immensely in my capacity to communicate with an audience, I'm a better teacher, and my judgement in complex matters of action is more fine tuned. I'm astonished at the sense I get in talking with people about retirement, people approaching retirement, even people who are in mid-career. I'm astonished at the kind of inner picture, inner image, of a uniform life trajectory that rises, then levels, then falls. And at my age of seventy-seven to see this image coming through in the conversation of someone in his or her fifties, it almost makes you laugh. I have to ask what that image is doing to them?

I think that people should begin to think, maybe in their late fifties, early sixties, how they want to deal with the phenomenon of age and work. Maybe their job stops, but they continue things they had done in an extracurricular way. They have hobbies. They have groups they're part of that won't stop. They should begin to cultivate the activities that won't end with retirement. The old rule is that if you haven't done something ten years before retirement you're probably not going to do much about it after retirement. Something that's going to be really interesting after retirement is likely to be something you became interested in much earlier.

I'm at peace with myself, but I'm still not totally at peace with my calendar. That's what I fight. But it's fun. I wouldn't want to stop. The world still makes a great many demands on me and I'm fighting those demands constantly, but I wouldn't like it if they stopped. I am making demands on the world. I still have a strong feeling that I would be able to say something that would be helpful.

I think there is something about these later years: a freedom from the scoreboard. You have the feeling when you're young that you've got to strive, to make it somehow, and that there is a scoreboard that will tell you how you're doing. I think that gets washed out as you get older. You don't need the merit badges any more, don't need the titles, the worldly things.

I think some people give up. They surrender, either to their life circumstances or to some inner sense of defeat, or just to the feeling, "Now I'm on the Western Slope of life." A friend of mine in his mid-sixties used that expression about himself, and I told him it was a *terrible* phrase to use! It sounds like you're riding off into the sunset. I think people develop a kind of "Well, it's over," attitude, and it is very hard on these people. The human organism is built to seek goals, significant goals: goals that engage the mind and the heart both.

My long term goal is to express as clearly as I can and as effectively as I can what I think this country has to face up to in its education. Its sense of social responsibility, the way it governs itself, I think we've got real problems. Our country needs to shape up. We enormously overvalue talent as against character, resilience, and endurance, which are the things that really make life work. One of my long term goals is to say that somehow, as clearly as I can, to as many people as I can. I'm still studying, trying to understand, so I can say it more clearly.

In my case, I find that my personal relationships are very rewarding and a great source of strength. My family is central to me. My wife and I have been married for fifty-six years. Our two daughters are very close to us, and so are our four grandchildren. That's been a very important thing in my life. You're giving and you're receiving. Plus, I have a network of friends for whom the same is true--long relationships of trust and affection and mutual support, which I find immensely rewarding.

Charles M. Schulz

CHAPTER THIRTEEN

Charles M. Schulz

Charles Schulz's comic strip, Peanuts, *is read by more than one hundred million people daily, in over two thousand newspapers, and in twenty-six different languages. Schulz and his progeny are the root of a marketing nexus spanning the last four decades and include entries in the world of television, movies, books, and children's products ranging from bedspreads to electric toothbrushes. 1990 marks the fortieth anniversary of the* Peanuts *characters.*

Schulz has twice won comic art's highest honor, the Reuben Award in 1955, and again in 1964. Snoopy and Charlie Brown went to the moon as mascots of the Apollo 10 astronauts in 1969. In 1987, the National Cartoonists Society presented Schulz with the Gold Brick Award as he was inducted into the Cartoonist Hall of Fame. Mr. Schulz went to Paris in January 1990, for the opening of a Peanuts *exhibit at the Louvre. He was named Commander in The Order of Arts and Letters, France's highest award for excellence in the arts.*

Also honoring the 40th anniversary, the Cartoon Museum in San Francisco is hosting a Peanuts *art exhibit, as well as the Smithsonian Museum.*

Charles Schulz is a native of Minnesota, and currently lives in Northern California with his wife, Jeannie.

———— ❖ ————

I don't regard my work as work. I regard it as equivalent to someone who plays the violin or does water colors or anything simply for his or her own enjoyment. In fact, I have almost a superstition about it in that I have never said that I cannot do something on such and such a day because I have to go to work. I always say I have to go to the studio. Somehow I have the feeling that if I start complaining that this is work, it will all be taken away from me. I have never called it work, even though I will admit that there are times when it is very hard work.

I do it because it's the only thing that I really know how to do and I think that I am an authority on comic strips. I don't think that I'm the greatest cartoonist who ever lived and I don't think *Peanuts* is necessarily the greatest comic strip that has ever existed, but I think I know more about drawing comic strips or as much as any person who's ever attempted to do them. So it has become my whole life. I don't think it was the greatest ambition in the world, but I've always been proud of the fact that I think I made the most of what abilities were given to me. I have a good combination of abilities and I don't think I have wasted what talents have been given to me, and that is something of which I've been reasonably proud.

It gives me great pleasure when I have a funny idea, one that I know is good, and when I am drawing and the lines are all falling into place, just the way I want them. It does give me a great deal of satisfaction, the same way as turning out a perfect water color, where all the brush strokes seem to fall in just the right place, or if somebody is playing an intricate piano or violin sonata and everything goes just right.

I come from the generation which was the first generation to be able to complete high school. My mother and father went only to the third grade. I doubt if my grandparents went even that far. I think I had one aunt who finished high school. I doubt if there were any of the others of that generation to go that far. Now, of course, the next generations as I look around, quite a few of them have gone on to college. My one son got a master's degree. But there was no driving pursuit of education in our family.

One of the things I've always been most grateful for was the fact that my mother and dad never stood in the way of this strange ambition that their son had. They did not try to influence me to go in some other directions. I think they were probably worried about it for a long while. My mother, of course, didn't live long enough. She died when she was 48 and I was only 20, so she did not live long enough to see the later struggles or the successes. But my dad did. He admitted that there was

a time even after I had signed my first contract and began to draw that he wondered if I was going to be able to think of enough ideas to keep on going. So he at least got to see it. I've always been grateful that they never attempted to stand in the way.

Now, I admired his own pursuits. I'm not ever sure of all the stories that we hear about our parents and grandparents are correct. But the story that I remember is that my dad worked on a farm in Nebraska pitching hay one summer to save enough money so that he could go to barber school, which he did. He eventually owned his own barber shop. That took a lot of ambition. And it was simply the lack of education that kept him from going even further. I remember people always saying to him, Schulz, they always called him Schulz, by his last name, you should have been a senator. He probably would have made a good senator. He was very much involved in barber politics for the advancement of the profession. But as far as encouraging me, they never stood in the way. He paid for the correspondence course that I finally took. I know he had trouble making the monthly payments, but he finally made them anyway. It used to worry me.

One of my early mentors was my Uncle Harris, who loved comic strips and was always interested in my career. He died of cancer after the war, a few years after World War II, and I had already gotten started. So he did see me sell the comic strip anyway, and I think that delighted him. But he was always interested in my career. He gave me support and encouragement.

I was always self-motivated. I certainly didn't get very much encouragement in school. I had one school teacher, I remember, who taught illustration, and I got very high grades from her, but beyond that none of the other teachers ever showed any interest in someone who could draw. In fact, they almost down-played it, especially if they saw that it was related to any type of cartooning.

Even though I might be drawing something that may have some social comment or content, it is still the drawing itself, the creation of the actual cartoon, the pen lines that make up the cartoon, the quality of the pen lines, the craftsmanship that is involved, the composition of the cartoon that is the real accomplishment. We have to forget about what the words are saying or things like that. Let's try to just talk about it as pictures, as drawings in the sand or drawings on the chalk board. The quality of the drawing itself is so important to me. This is what I think real cartoonists admire. Not so much what the characters have

said and things like that but good cartoonists admire other cartoonists simply for the quality of the pen lines and the drawing itself. This doesn't mean literal draftsmanship always, but there's a certain warmth, there is the craftsmanship involved there beyond illustrative quality. The man that used to draw *Popeye* for instance, was not a great artist. The man that drew *Krazy Kat.* You don't see illustrative quality there necessarily but you see wonderful pen and ink work. The man that used to draw *Napoleon, Skippy*, Roy Crane who used to draw *WashTubbs* and *Captain Easy*, Milt Coniff, who drew the early *Terry and the Pirates* strips, and many others, there's a quality there beyond what was going on in the feature that is so admired by other cartoonists. And this is what I think you are really after day to day, just trying to do something that is really good. Of course, then it is what the characters do and say that the public seems to like. That's another step, and if people like what you're doing and saying, then you've accomplished something more.

It never ends. Not only because of your search for excellence, but then there's also all the wonderful things that happen to you. If I had stopped drawing ten years ago, I never would have found myself with an exhibit in the Louvre. And who knows what's going to happen if I keep going for another ten years. I have the advantage of being able to take part in a lot of different elements in cartooning: books, movies, television shows, interviews like this, which are just fascinating, that's all.

I own, within two blocks of my studio, what is regarded as the world's most beautiful ice arena. It enables me to be surrounded daily by people of all ages. One of the best things about it is the mixture of ages, so that we are not confined with our own age groups all day long every day. I think that's a tragedy. But I will admit, for the last almost ten years now, to looking at younger people and envying them when I see them running down the street. I look at little children and I think, gee, it would be nice to be a little kid again, to be able to start all over again. Although I didn't necessarily enjoy being a little kid. I hated the things that little kids had to go through. But I do admire the young person that I see jogging along the street and seeing how freely they run and see the muscles in their arms and legs flowing and their flat stomachs.

I first noticed something going wrong when I was probably in my late 40's. I used to play ball with my two sons friends all the time. I was

playing third base one day, and somebody hit a hot grounder between me and third base and I bent over to get it and it just zoomed right on by me. Suddenly I realized that I could not bend as fast as I could have done even five years before that. Years later, just a few years ago, I thought I'd play with our arena softball team, which is composed mainly of young people who work around the arena in their 20's. I discovered that I could not follow the flight of the fly balls like I could when I was young. Suddenly, the ball was out of focus and I couldn't follow it like I used to be able to. And so I gave up. It was a setback, I don't enjoy that sort of thing.

I suppose my greatest tragedy thus far was the loss of my mother, who died after suffering terribly from cancer for some time. I think I turned 20 when I got my first draft notice and she was dying then, but I could recall a year or two before that when I would awaken at night hearing her crying from the pain. It was all so frustrating. Then suddenly getting drafted and saying good night to her one night. She said, I suppose we should say goodbye because we'll probably never see each other again. And it was true. She died the next day. And I was allowed to come home on a ten-day furlough for the funeral and then return to camp. That was a pretty low day.

If it had any religious significance, it was a religious experience of gratitude for the spiritual help of being able to survive this. 40-50 years later I look back upon it and I suppose the only way we can really judge our own experiences is to place one experience over another so they overlap. And I think about what to me was the low point of my life and at the very same time there were people being herded into boxcars in Germany and Poland and other places undergoing experiences which were infinitely worse than mine. But we can't really compare these things because we all go through experiences according to where we are, and who we are, and what we are. But it enable us to draw a few parallels. I came out of the war as a staff sergeant. Here I was just a young guy who noboby ever thought would amount to much. But I went in with a bunch of men and I became a man. I became the squad leader of a light machine gun squad, which was what I wanted. I finally wanted to be a good soldier. And I worked hard at it. Those were hard times.

I have always been thankful for the abilities that I have been given, and I have always refused to sell them out. This is putting aside something I suppose people would call commercialism. There are some that think I've sold out because I advertise for insurance companies. But besides all that, I have never used my ability to draw anything that you would consider immoral or a dirty cartoon or anything like that. I've always tried to draw things that were decent and uplifting. And the most perfect example of that was the book that I wrote in 1963 called *Happiness Is a Warm Puppy*, a book that was just totally innocent and nice and yet was the number one bestseller of the year. Something that people would say couldn't be done. Our play, *You're a Good Man, Charlie Brown*, a play which is totally innocent and nice and decent and fun and all of that, is the most performed musical in the history of the American theatre. Not a curse word in the whole thing. Not a raunchy scene in the whole thing. It's all uplifting and good. This has been my pledge to whoever it is that creates us, whatever we want to call Him, that's been my pledge to do the best with what talent has been given me.

I suppose I've matured in certain attitudes in that I don't care so much what other people think about me any more. I find myself more at ease with people in that I don't have to try to impress anybody anymore. I find that I have more friends now. I find that I get along much better with women now than I ever have in my life. I enjoy talking with them and I have lunch quite frequently over at the arena with different ladies, whether it's an interview or just somebody who likes to ice skate. I enjoy that. I'm much more at ease with women than I was years and years ago. I suppose most men feel that way.

I talked to a group of seventh graders yesterday, which I normally would never do. I just don't like going out making appearances like that. But I told them that if they were lucky, most likely they would probably live to be about 70 years old. And I said if you're going to live to 70, that means you're going to have to get up on a lot of Monday mornings. So I said you better pick out something that you're going to do the rest of your life where you can look forward to Monday mornings, which is what I do. I like coming to the studio where I'm in control. I like seeing what's going to be in the morning mail and I like what I do. And so I told these children that this is what they'd better do. Don't pay any attention to what anybody tells you, whether it's a teacher or parent or grandparent or somebody like that. Do and be what you want to be because you're going to have to face a lot of Monday mornings.

From a physical standpoint, I wouldn't have the slightest idea why

some people age better than others. I suppose that has a lot to do with heredity. Not being medically intelligent I wouldn't have any idea. Now, I have never smoked a cigarette in my life. I don't have the slightest idea what the feeling would be, which is incredible going through three years in the Army. I had to eat Milky Ways and lost several teeth because of it. I've never drank. I never had a drink in my life until the third year in the Army. Somebody talked me into having a daiquiri. Even now I just don't drink at all. I could tolerate a half an inch of wine, I suppose, when everybody else is drinking. Interest in sports, I suppose, has a lot to do with it. I've always stayed reasonably active. Right now, I'm having a hard time doing it. I've got to get back at it and do some more. I played hockey last night for an hour. I had a lot of fun, but my back hurts this morning. I scored about five goals.

The trait of a cartoonist is to be able to see the humor in the tragedies that Man has to face. People say, how do you think of those funny ideas? I say, I'm very clever. I'm reasonably witty. I was astounded about three or four months ago, I received a letter from a very close friend. We were in the same platoon and we spent a lot of time together. And he said that he just thought it was about time that he wrote to me and just tell me how much he appreciated the friendship that he and I had during those years together. He said, you made me laugh. Well, it never occurred to me that I had made anybody laugh. I was certainly not the life of the party. I've never been that kind. That was the first I had heard from him since we were discharged. What he said made me feel good. It was something that never occurred to me.

I have no plans right now to stop drawing the strip. So the strip has always been the main thing. The strip has sort of been the hub of the wheel. I hope to be able to continue to draw the strip and make it not only as good as it's ever been but I always hope everyday to make it better. I wish that I could think of a good idea to make another movie. We've done four movies. I haven't been totally satisfied with them. I had one wonderful idea for a movie which turned into an hour television show, but was a disappointment because it didn't get made the way I wanted it to. That would be one ambition, I would like to be able to do some writing but I'm not sure I'm capable of it. I'm not sure that I really am a writer. I have a son who writes very well and I don't think I can ever write as well as he can. But I would like to write, I don't know if I could write a novel or not.

Portraits of Passion: Aging, Defying the Myth

I live always with the hope that my children will achieve what they want and will be happy and will not have to suffer any great tragedies in their lives. We have ten grandchildren now and I hope that they all will remain healthy and everything will work out well for them. I hope that I don't outlive all of them. My grandmother had nine children and outlived six of them, which I think is one of the great tragedies of life. She was an old lady her whole life and saw so much sadness. Yet she laughed a lot.

PART THREE

The Life of Service

Rollo May

CHAPTER FOURTEEN

Rollo May

Rollo May received his A.B. from Oberlin College in 1930. He received a M.A. Divinity from Union Theological Seminary cum laude in 1939 and his Ph.D. from Columbia University summa cum laude in 1949. His book The Art of Counseling *was published in 1939, and was the first book in the whole field. Since that time he has written* The Meaning of Anxiety *(1950),* Man's Search For Himself *(1953),* Existential Psychology *(1961),* Love and Will *(1969) for which he received the Ralph Waldo Emerson Award,* Power and Innocence *for which he received the Martin Luther King Award (1972),* The Courage to Create *(1975),* The Discovery of Being *(1983),* My Quest For Beauty *(1985), and many papers in the field. He is a Supervisory and Training Analyst of the William Alanson White Institute of Psychiatry, Psychology and Psychoanalysis.*

He has received numerous honorary degrees, notably the Award for the Outstanding Contribution to the Profession of Psychology by the American Psychological Association.

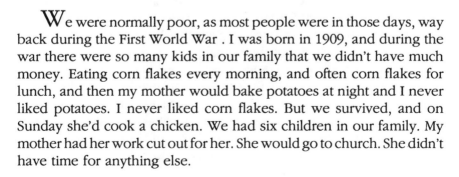

We were normally poor, as most people were in those days, way back during the First World War . I was born in 1909, and during the war there were so many kids in our family that we didn't have much money. Eating corn flakes every morning, and often corn flakes for lunch, and then my mother would bake potatoes at night and I never liked potatoes. I never liked corn flakes. But we survived, and on Sunday she'd cook a chicken. We had six children in our family. My mother had her work cut out for her. She would go to church. She didn't have time for anything else.

Portraits of Passion: Aging, Defying the Myth

My father was a YMCA secretary. He liked his work. My father was a role model for me in his way. He liked people. He liked to tell jokes to his friends. He was very outgoing, and he was always liked by other people, too. He never made much money, I think $3000 a year was the highest he ever made. I didn't at that time like the kind of work he did, except I got a chance to go off to camp in the summer time, which was good. My father influenced me to be interested in religion. He was not terribly sophisticated, but I did learn from my father to be responsible and be honest.

Paul Tillich was my mentor-father. He was more of a mentor to me than all other men put together, Tillich was very different from my father. He, a German, came over to this country in 1934. I had been in Europe long enough to garner great respect for German scholars.

Being in Europe and my close association with Tillich changed my direction. Tillich and I became friends and we remained that way until he died. Tillich was one of the five great philosophers in Europe; most of them were German. He was the one from whom I learned most of all in my life.

I did apply at Columbia, but they then scarcely knew the names of Adler and Jung. The psychologists at Columbia said nothing at all during their lectures about these men. When I had asked them afterward about these men, they said they weren't psychologists. To be a psychologist in those days meant you had to teach dogs how to salivate. Nobody knew anything about psychotherapy; the colleges weren't too concerned about philosophy. Of course, that was just at the time of the Great Depression.

When I decided to go to Union Seminary, it was not because I wanted to be a minister. Rather I wanted to study anxiety, tragedy and the meaning of life. It was the only place you could study these subjects; there was practically no philosophy taught in this country. I had a marvelous time at Union Seminary. The professors there weren't concerned about orienting us to the local church. They were concerned about suffering, love, about the human condition.

I think that since the First World War, we have been in a progressively lower moral state. Tillich was exiled by Hitler, along all of the other great Germans, such as Thomas Mann. The Second World War was a terrible thing: the bombing of Dresden, the killing , and the whole concept of the concentration camps. It didn't show the nobility of man. Now I think our society , ever since the First World War, has been in a state of growing dishonesty. You see it. It used to be that when man dropped a quarter, somebody would run after him with it. Now in New York you can't go out after dark. You get bumped even on Central Park West. I think it's terrible.

I think that those persons who age well are those who love their work, like so many of the musicians or the artists - like Toscanini for example. They age well because they have something challenging. They create; they still possess a love for life as they age. Now I think that's very important.

The work I do is as full an expression of my total abilities as possible. When I write, I get insights, I talk with people who know something about what I write about. And all of this put together is what I call work. Now, I never liked to do work; I have done several jobs where I just had to hang on by my teeth. It used to be said when I was back at Oberlin College that I would give anything in the world or pay any amount of money, in order to be able to do the job which I get paid for.

I don't have time to die. I love to paint. I still love women, and I'm very fond of a number of women who are my good friends. I like to talk intensively with my colleagues about problems that we are concerned about. I enjoy my own feelings, as well as others in my life.

In summers we go to New Hampshire. There are five lakes I see when driving to the store from our house on Lake Winnepsaukee. That's great, I love living there. The best thing for me is to write . My book, called *My Quest for Beauty*, has prints of my paintings and drawings, I like this area of life.

What I don't like is the great advertising, and the commercialism of California. I think we've got enough things, and I don't think life is made up of the amount of things a person has anyway. Many people write about making a million dollars; what are they going to do with it? They go on trips, and overeat, and walk around foreign countries that they haven't made the time to read about. I think that our excessive loving of life in the sense of being entertained is surely wrong. I think the only thing you entertain is your sense of boredom.

I've worked for 7 or 8 years on this present book on mythology, and it's a temporary goal. I think that the larger goal is the intensity of living. We don't know where we go or what happens afterwards, but we don't need to know in any case.

Lionel J. Wilson

CHAPTER FIFTEEN

Lionel J. Wilson

Mayor Wilson was born in New Orleans, Louisiana, the eldest of eight children. During World War Two, he served as a First Sergeant in the European theater and was honorably discharged in 1945.

He received his BA degree in Economics from the University of California at Berkeley in 1939, and his Juris Doctor from Hastings College of Law in 1949. In 1960, Governor Edmund G. Brown Sr. appointed him to the Oakland-Piedmont Municipal Court. He was elevated to the Alameda County Superior Court in 1964. He became presiding judge of that court in 1973.

In 1977, Mayor Wilson was elected as the first black mayor of Oakland. Since his election he has served on the board of directors of the League of California Cities, various committees of the U.S. Conference of Mayors, and the National League of Cities. Following his 1977 election, Wilson was appointed by Governor Edmund G. Brown Jr. to the State Comprehensive Employment Training Act program (CETA). He was appointed by President Carter to the commission to select judges for the United States Court of Patents and Appeals. He is a past president and founding member of the board of directors of the New Oakland Committee, and still retains his membership in a law firm. Wilson has received nationwide accolades for his attention to issues involving minorities, youth, the disabled, the elderly, the homeless, and the unemployed.

———❖———

Portraits of Passion: Aging, Defying the Myth

I believe that there are just certain people whose personality and make-up is such that they wouldn't be happy just sitting around doing nothing. My wife and I have talked about it. I'm very active in tennis, and I'm just starting to learn to play golf. But, as she said, I wouldn't be happy just sitting around playing tennis and golf. In addition to that, I believe that there are things that I would still like to do. There are many things that I would like to do.

My parents had 8 children, I was the oldest of 8. We were all taught to sustain ourselves and contribute to our family. I guess I was 10 when I started with a paper route. You had to do your own collecting, you didn't just serve the papers. By the time I was 12 I was working in my uncle's barbershop. He had a big four-chair shop on 8th between Broadway and Washington in Oakland. I was working in there everyday after school and on Saturdays. In our family, the work ethic was something that our parents felt was important. It was necessary at the time. It was later translated into the same kind of activity in terms of those things that I believed in, those types of activities where I felt that there was a need and I might make some kind of a contribution.

When I walk around the city, I remember the city in terms of what it was 13, 14 years ago. The downtown had lost many of the small businesses through redevelopment. Here in this city-center area there were two new buildings, the Clorox Building and the bank building. Those were the only buildings. There were hopes and plans that had been on the burner for a long time and hadn't been fulfilled. I felt that there was a great potential in this city. I love this city of Oakland. So I eventually decided that I could make a difference in terms of the development of the city.

There was a man who had a small business of his own selling cosmetics. He also distributed black newspapers, *The Pittsburgh Courier* and *The Chicago Defender*. The only local paper then was *The California Voice*. He was a customer in my uncle's barbershop. He was someone who was vitally interested in politics and active in politics. He would talk to me from time to time. He was a great philosopher and he was constantly philosophizing on different things that were important in terms of how one lives. I felt he was a very wise man.

Probably the smartest politician I've ever known was D.G. Gibson. He lived in South Berkeley. Then there was the pharmacist in Berkeley, the late Bryan Rumford, Assemblyman. I used to deliver some of my papers in Berkeley, and I would go into his pharmacy and talk with him. I greatly admired him as a politician, but I never saw myself as one who might become active in terms of seeking political office.

I'm 75. Like most families, we had tragedies. We lost a brother, the fourth brother was the navigator of a B-17 lost in World War II, but there was no other particular tragedy in my life. I think that in terms of how I view the aging process, somewhere along the line, a long time ago, I developed a philosophy that it's necessary that one learn and appreciate that life is a constantly changing process. It changes from day to day, and year to year, from the cradle to the grave. The happiest people are those people who learn and appreciate that fact.

I grew up in meager circumstances, as most did. But now I suppose that my wife and I have planned well, and economically I'm in a very stable situation. We're comfortable financially. We can do pretty much what we want to do, what we like to do. My wife and I are both very active physically, so I suppose the difference in the near future is that I'm going to have more time to do things for myself, with my family. I'm already involved in the development of a program around a YMCA where I once worked.

There's too great an emphasis on age today. We see it in so many different ways. The media and people just seem to be too ready to lay down and put everything aside. Too many people think in terms of age. Too many people worry about the aging factor. Too many people don't take care of themselves physically and don't understand that it's a long road. I believe in doing most things in moderation, except sports. One has to develop a kind of mentality that sees the aging process as something that is an individual factor in one's life. It depends upon the kind of life one leads, and barring any unforeseen serious illness or accident.

About 15 or 20 years ago, while I was on the superior court, I had the assignment to handle the psychiatric calendar. Which meant every morning I would go in and I would be presented with a stack of files. I'd go through the files, and these were the people who were appearing before the court for psychiatric reasons on that morning. It was a constant source of amazement to me that I would have gone over, for instance File A, then the person who was represented in that file walked into the room. That person may have been 50, and walked into the room looking like 80. The next person might have been 75, and walked into the room looking like 50. The one thing I learned in that process was the incredible difference in the way people age. I just don't believe that chronological age is that much a factor, at least in the way I approach life. I have to laugh at myself every once in a while because I refer to some people as elderly or old people, and I'm older than they are.

I don't think that there's any particular trait that serves a person better than having a strong self-discipline. I had lawyers say to me when I walked off the bench, "My God, what patience you have, judge." Or say to someone else, god, Judge Wilson has such tremendous patience. I've heard the same thing in presiding over these council meetings with hoards of people in there week after week. I always laugh and say, that's not patience, that's discipline. I think that can be a factor which can serve one well in any kind of activity or any kind of endeavor. When one runs into roadblocks, or problems of one kind or another, it helps to understand that they're not always going to be there. There is a tomorrow and if you apply yourself to whatever the challenges are, you can usually achieve a certain amount of success. You can't win them all. You do what you can when you face each challenge and then move on.

William Laurence Gee

CHAPTER SIXTEEN

William Laurence Gee

Dr. Gee was born in Canton, China on August 27, 1914. He became a naturalized citizen of the United States in 1943. He served in the Armed Forces as a Staff Sergeant with a Cryptography unit during the Second World War in the China-Burma-India campaign. Dr. Gee is a widower, and has four children. He received his education at the University of San Francisco, University of Washington, acquired his D.D.S. from the College of Dentistry of the University of California, and later completed a residency in Oral Surgery.

He was one of the founders and organizers of the On Lok Senior Health Services *for long-term care of elderly invalids. This program has been the model for PACE (Program of All-inclusive Care for the Elderly) on a national level.*

Dr. Gee has received many appointments and awards for his outstanding community work, among these honors are: Public Health Dentist, National Advisory Committee, 1981 White House Conference on Aging; President, San Francisco Commission on Aging; Phoebe Apperson Hearst Medallion (Most Distinguished Ten of the Bay Area); Chinese American Citizens Alliance Award; United Way Voluntary Award; The Phillip Burton Award for Distinguished Service; University of California - San Francisco Award; 1990 Alumnae of the Year Award: UCSF.

---------- ❖ ----------

My professional life came to me rather late compared to most dentists that have gone into their professional career. I went into dental school after World War II, after service in the Army.

Before the war, when I came here as a young boy, we had to rely upon ourselves to stay alive. We had to work to eat, to live. At a very early age I started working as a houseboy. My Dad couldn't work so I had to, that is the way it was. You can't blame everything on somebody else.

I was one of the few lucky ones that were able to come to the United States. I left millions and millions of my counterparts in China to come to the United States for an education. I never forgot that. In the beginning I was reminded of that by my father. But after that, when I received news from China telling me of the difficulties they were having, mine didn't seem too big.

My Grandfather came over here and established himself as a Chinese herbalist/ doctor in the 1870's. In the old days, the Chinese laborers didn't believe in Western medicine and they didn't feel comfortable with the general practitioners. So they relied on their traditional medical help whenever they could. My Grandfather use to carry his apothecary along with him, in a big box full of herbs. So he made a fairly good living, but he couldn't bring his family over. In those days immigration was very precarious and the laws were very restrictive. But he could bring his male offsprings, sons, over to carry on the family business. In fact, that's how I came over.

I could come over, but my Mother couldn't. I never saw my mother after 6 years old. We corresponded by letter. After I came over then you had the Great Depression where nobody had any money and there was barely enough to send home. We were just keeping alive so I did not have the luxury of going back to the old country.

I thought that the WPA in the depression was a great thing. Even though my family was not eligible for any of the benefits. Aliens weren't allowed to join a WPA. But it was one way to get a country out of the depression and create jobs for them. That's why I keep wondering now, how come someone in Washington hasn't had that idea? As a nation, we have many homeless, and jobless.

I was placed in a Baptist home for Chinese boys. We were given religious education, but our schooling was in public schools. After a few years, when I was physically able to, I became a houseboy for a very kind neurologist. He and his wife had no children, so I was their houseboy and adopted son. He kept saying that you should take advantage of the opportunity and go to medical school. He said when it's time to go, if I'm around I'll help you. He encouraged me to look at his textbooks and his technical books. He passed away before I graduated from high school.

I feel I owe a lot of people favors that helped me on my way, like the doctor, Rossner Graham. In my mind I don't owe anybody anything, but I feel that if somebody was kind to me then I should repay the favor. One of the better payoffs for me is when I go down to On Lok Senior Health Services and watch the participants. I see people that I grew up with who are there now as participants, as patients. Inside I say to myself, if it wasn't for me doing my little bit, they wouldn't be as comfortable as they are now.

Physically I can't do as much anymore, but mentally I can still do it. The sort of skill that I can contribute now to the general welfare of the community is that I now know my way around Washington, around Sacramento, around City Hall in San Francisco. Because of my knowledge, quite often I can get things done without creating a lot of waves. It took a lifetime to learn my way around. I did make mistakes on the way. I say to myself, I shouldn't have said that to that guy. I should've been nicer to him. Not because I liked him or anything like that, but because it may come back and haunt me. That's politics.

As I look back, people used to have better manners, were more courteous to each other. They were more willing to stop and help you. I don't mind people asking me to do something for them, after all they're only doing what I used to be doing myself. So I can't fault them. The only thing is I have to be careful. I can turn them down without making an enemy of them.

When my dad got sick, we couldn't pay doctors' bills, hospital bills, drug bills, we couldn't pay anything. Somehow or other they were forgiven, or they were allowed to slide by and written off. My dad got cured. I felt that I should pay it back someway.

I felt at that time that probably I would not be able to pay them back in monetary ways, but I could help build the new Chinese hospital. I was in on the fundraising. At one time when they were ready to close up the hospital, I went and represented the Chinese hospital and was able to convince the panel that the hospital, although small, served a very useful purpose. It helped when I found out that the chairman of the panel was somebody I knew, Father Flynn of the San Francisco Catholic Church.

As people get older, there's an inclination for them to slack off.

Portraits of Passion: Aging, Defying the Myth

They think that they are not capable of doing everything. Well, you can recognize that fact but you don't have to give in to it entirely. That's one lesson I learned from reading Walter Reuther, that when you're fighting in a union battle you have to outstay your opponent. I followed the lead of the people that had a hand in creating the destiny of this country. You can't overlook the union leaders, people in the union movement like Walter Reuther.

My long term goal is that the things I started, will continue and become permanent. My work is kind of a life substance for me. I've already retired from dentistry, but I haven't retired from life. It's a way of keeping in touch with the rest of the world. When I keep on doing what I have been doing, I stay alive. I don't vegetate. I have an interest in living. It is a selfish reason.

The people who age well are the ones that seem to have a purpose in life, whether it's a selfish one or a non-selfish one, it doesn't matter. But if they have that interest within themselves, they will age well. The one that doesn't have a purpose in life will just get up in the morning and say, oh, another day, go read the paper.

I tell myself you can't get things done overnight. Some things you can, but most things you can't. So don't get frustrated. You just bide your time, but be ready for that time to come. You've got to remember one thing. The underdog in the political scene in the United States doesn't stay an underdog all the time. Eventually, they'll come to the surface. If you believe in the people you picked, don't despair, don't give up.

In looking back I think I should have paid more attention to my wife when she was alive. I think I should have catered to her a little bit more. I often wonder whether I could've done more. She was home alone quite often while I was out at meetings or off to Washington to lobby for whatever we needed. I often wonder why we can't all be like Elizabeth and Bob Dole, both of them are involved.

A. W. Clausen

CHAPTER SEVENTEEN

A.W. Clausen

Born in Hamilton, Illinois in 1923, Mr. Clausen earned a B.A. degree from Carthage College in 1944, and a J.D. from the University of Minnesota in 1949. He holds honorary degrees from Carthage College, Gonzaga University, Lewis and Clark College, University of Notre Dame, University of the Pacific, and the University of Santa Clara.

A.W. Clausen is a director and Chairman of the Executive Committees of the Board of Directors of BankAmerica Corporation and its wholly owned subsidiary, Bank of America N.T.& S.A. Previously, he was Chairman and Chief Executive Officer of the corporation and the bank. He retired from those posts in 1990.

Mr. Clausen joined the bank in 1949 and was elected President and Chief Executive officer in 1970. He left the bank in 1981 to become President of the World Bank, a position he retained until 1986.

Currently he serves as a member of the Advisory Boards or Councils of the Harvard Business School; Stanford Graduate School of Business; the University of California School of Business and the University of Southern California School of Business. He is also a member of the Board of Overseers of the University of California, San Francisco and a Trustee of Carthage College. He is a member of the International Monetary Conference, the Brookings Institute, the Committee for Economic Development, the Overseas Development Council, as well as numerous other professional and humanitarian organizations.

Portraits of Passion: Aging, Defying the Myth

Mr. Clausen has received awards from the governments of Italy, Japan, Senegal, South Korea, Spain, and Venezuela. In 1979, he was named California industrialist of the Year.

My feeling is that I can make a contribution to society, including the global society. It's a natural thing to do, in a very modest way, to share my experiences. That's why I keep on working. As an example, in three weeks my schedule takes me to Linz, Austria to participate in a forum with ministers of finance and bankers of central and eastern European countries. We will discuss how to transform the individual economies of these countries from a centrally planned and controlled approach to a market economy that follows the invisible hand of the marketplace, Adam Smith-style.

At BankAmerica earlier this year, we did an analysis of the Central and Eastern European countries and the Soviet Union. I drew on that at a conference in the Soviet Union dealing with how to integrate the Soviets into the global economy. It was worth participating in that conference because the economy is the biggest issue in the Soviet Union today and, indeed, a very important one for the rest of the world as well. I hope there are things one can contribute after being CEO for 16 years of a major financial institution, BankAmerica Corporation, and President of the World Bank for five years.

As for my background, I am the product of a middle-income family, poor financially, but rich in the important things. My father was born in Norway, so I'm first-generation. My mother was also first generation. My grandmother, from my mother's side, came from what is now Poland. Neither of my parents had a college degree. My father did attend college, but he couldn't graduate because he got called into the service. Maybe that's why my parents' big ambition for the family was to have their children become college graduates, and it happened.

My father was editor, publisher and owner of a weekly newspaper in Hamilton, Illinois, a little town of 1800 people. It was a family operation, and my first job at 10 years old was standing on a box feeding presses. So I learned a trade and how to work. My father also taught me to have a global perspective. We had a big house in Hamilton, on the outskirts of town. We spent a lot of time in the kitchen in the winter, gathered around a wood-burning stove in the kitchen. Some of my fondest memories are of listening to my father talk. He'd tell me about Europe and World War I, in which he fought. Listening to those stories about his upbringing in Norway made me interested in global geography. So, out of respect and admiration for my father, my goal was to be a global citizen, a transnational citizen, even at that early age.

I've tried to pass on this lesson. In 1977, my travels took me back to my home town to give a lecture, a convocation to the high school students. I told them that not too many blocks from that community high school, in the same building as my high school, my teachers taught me about international affairs. The world is becoming increasingly interdependent, and it's shrinking. Therefore, an awareness of the world is beneficial, it's helpful. That's ingrained in me, and my father is to thank for it.

My father was also part of a discussion group that met every month. The group's members used to gather in our home periodically, and I would tune in from upstairs, listening to the conversations. One night, it was in the 30's, I remember hearing them discussing the theory of evolution and those kinds of esoteric subjects. This was from a group that lived in a hog and corn community - that was the principle livelihood in that part of the world.

Growing up, I worked my way through college, as did many students. I admired and respected the owner and publisher of the *Carthage College Journal.* My job was to run the linotype part-time for him during summers and also during school. There were many other people that good fortune sent my way who I respected and admired, such as my high school English teacher, Thelma Davis. I can still remember my first grade teacher leaving an impact on my life, too. Her name was Miss Kindred.

My college major was philosophy, but Uncle Sam called me to duty during World War II. It was a few months before my graduation in March of 1943. Had the service waited until June, I would have graduated then, but that had to wait until my return in 1944. During school, my appetite for reading was prodigious. Some of my favorites were Plato and Aristotle, and considering the real "truths" of the world. Ethics and principles mean a lot to me. They are something I've always tried to live by and encourage in others.

There are always new things to learn in this area. For instance, in preparing for a recent lecture commemorating the 200th anniversary of the death of Adam Smith, I had an opportunity to read his *Wealth of Nations* again. I discovered that its message is really apolitical, and amoral. It didn't have a moral bias to it. However, my speech suggested that we have an opportunity - especially in Central and Eastern Europe - to inject a moral dimension into traditional capitalism.

My lectures on business ethics have also been delivered to groups in Washington, D.C. At Bank of America, we also had a two-day seminar on ethics for 300 of our senior officers. It was an important exercise for everyone involved. I guess this is all part of being a philosophy major; it transcends my business life.

How does one keep on going? You don't let things get you down. You do your best - always. You execute it and don't think about it, unless there are some mistakes that you can learn from. "Stay busy" is my motto. It has been all my life. Expect to stay busy, have more to do than you can possibly master. At the moment, my schedule keeps me quite busy, but I've always been in over my head. It's better that way.

My bank duties do not include day-to-day responsibilities. role allows me to choose what to become involved with. Raising money for good causes, working in the community, being a vice chairman of Bay Vision 20-20, trying to figure out the kind of environment which is most desirable for the Bay Area - all of these things are important to me.

Looking back, I feel lucky. I am very grateful to have had the right parents, the right genes, and to have married the right lady. But staying active, being alert, and challenging yourself will add to your life - not shorten it.

I don't think of myself all that often. My goal has always been to think of others. That means doing your homework. People can rely on me to be prepared, and not shoot from the hip. So, my comments on a given subject are likely to be well thought out. My objective has always been to live up to my word and keep promises. Therefore, my perception of myself is someone who is very trustworthy. You can rely on my word, you can count on it.

I want to feel retired, but I don't. My schedule has kept me from taking off for two consecutive weeks, long enough to just relax with my wife and do nothing, not have to answer the phone and run through the daily routine. That doesn't bother me, in truth, I prefer to keep very busy. Maybe that will change when I get old, but I'm not old yet.

Mildred W. Levin

CHAPTER EIGHTEEN

Mildred W. Levin

Mildred W. Levin is a native San Franciscan. She attended the University of California at Berkeley, received the degree of Juris Doctor from Hastings College of Law in 1934. Mrs. Levin has devoted many years of her law practice to obtaining equal rights for, and the elimination of discrimination against women.

In 1974, Queen's Bench, an organization of lawyers and now a Bar Association, members Jettie Selvig, Mildred W. Levin, and the late Judge Agnes O'Brien, on behalf of Queen's Bench, established the Queen's Bench Foundation to study rape. On behalf of Queen's Bench as an amicus curiae, *Mrs. Levin successfully argued before the Supreme Court in the case of* The State of California vs. Rincon-Pineda, *which led to a judgement eliminating the cautionary instruction in rape cases that had discriminated against women since the seventeenth century.*

Mrs. Levin has been involved in many public service activities, namely President of Women Variety Club, Tent 32; Helpers for the Mentally Retarded; member of the Business and Professional Women's Club of San Francisco; member of NOW; and a member of The National Women's Political Caucus and The Native Daughters of the Golden West, Golden Gate Parlor Number 158. She was the recipient of a Certificate of Honor from the San Francisco Centennial Committee of the National Association of Women Lawyers. She was awarded the 1975 National Association of Women's Lawyers' Award; and the Special Award of Queen's Bench

Portraits of Passion: Aging, Defying the Myth

for her significant contribution to the International Women's Year 1975. She received a Recognition of Experience Certificate as a Trial Lawyer from the California Trial Lawyers Association.

Mrs. Levin is a widow, and has three children.

My father was born in Austria. He came here about 1898 as a very young man. My father believed in working and helping people. My father supported his father and mother in the old country, until they were murdered by the Russian soldiers in World War I. My mother, like myself, was born in San Francisco of a generation that had a strong fundamental work ethic.

I remember once being a judge in a speaking contest where the speaker talked about work. The audience thought that anyone who wanted to work was foolish. There was one woman speaker who said that whenever they wanted to punish convicts, they took away their right to work. There's no greater privilege in the world than the right to work.

As an attorney, I have been able to help people. This gives me a sense of satisfaction. I think that women in this society have a very difficult time, especially in dissolution (divorce) cases. Women generally do not have the earning capacity of men, and under this no-fault equal division law, the family home is usually sold and the woman does not have an opportunity to buy another house because usually she cannot qualify for a loan.

I would like to see the law changed in the dissolution cases.The court should have the discretion to give the family home to the wife in a long-term marriage. If the house is sold and the wive receives her share of the proceeds, many of the women trying to buy another house can't qualify for a loan because they don't have the earning capacity of men.

My husband passed away several years ago from Alzheimer's disease. We had three children. One daughter is a Superior Court Judge in San Francisco, the other daughter is a real estate agent and my son is a San Francisco police inspector. We were strict parents. My husband and I just expected my children to obey and they did. Children come to live with you, you don't come to live with them.

Every person has had personal tragedies. One of the greatest is when somebody you love has Alzheimer's Disease for eight years and when my first-born child passed away as an infant. I remember that my father used to say, "Do the best you can," and I always did the best I could. That's all that can be expected of anyone and this belief helped me overcome these terrible experiences.

There was an experience I had when I went out to practice law. I was twenty-two years of age, and there was a tremendous amount of prejudice against women. I remember going to one law firm seeking a job, the attorney kept me waiting there from 9 a.m. until 6 p.m. and never did see me. That experience made me a better person, because I have never turned anyone down I could help. I will let an experience teach me a lesson, but I won't let an experience make me bitter. One has to be a survivor. I believe in the Ten Commandments and the Golden Rule. These beliefs give me a standard for life, a moral code. I've tried to instill these principles in my children.

When I was a very young attorney another attorney gave me some bad advice on a case I was trying. He and other attorneys expected me to lose the case. I heard them snickering when I told the judge what the law was. The judge was a wonderful man and didn't want to embarrass me. He decided the case in my favor, and then said, "Mildred, go into my chambers and tell me what code section you're talking about." That taught me a lesson: don't rely on another person.

I think that people get things very easy today. Proper values are no longer being instilled in children like they used to be. I remember the Bank of America used to have a savings program. Every Friday after class you'd put in 25 cents into your account to build up a savings account. Because we live in a very affluent society today, children are not taught the value of savings.

People are living longer today, our whole concept of age is changing. Few people are going to be able to retire early and live decently. They have to keep abreast of the times, work and have hobbies. It's very important to exercise, take vitamins and maintain a healthy diet and be thankful for being alive.

People let themselves get old. They lose interest in life. Women let themselves get dependent on their husband. When he dies and they're left alone, they don't know how to adjust. They have become completely dependent on somebody. You come into the world alone and you go out of the world alone. Older people let themselves get lazy. St. Theresa once said, "The more you pamper your body, the more it wants to be pampered."

If you have an interest in life and you're independent, you'll age much better than somebody who's completely dependent on somebody else. I've always been a self-motivator. When I went out to practice law, that was considered one of the worst things a woman could do. Then I got married and practiced law, and that was considered terrible. Then when I raised my family and practiced law this was a disgrace. Then along came World War II and the whole world changed. Women started to go out to work, and they liked the standard of life they were able to maintain and refused to go back into the home.

I've always loved people. I'm sort of like Will Rogers: I've never met a person I didn't like. I will always remember what Justice Sandra Day O'Connor of the United States Supreme Court said, "when you leave this world you should be able to say to yourself, I've made this world a little better place."

Norman Cousins

CHAPTER NINETEEN

Norman Cousins

Norman Cousins is Adjunct Professor in the School of Medicine at the University of California, Los Angeles. For 25 years he was the editor of the Saturday Review *Magazine. He has authored 25 books including:* Head First: The Biology of Hope, The Pathology of Power, The Healing Heart, Anatomy of an Illness, Human Options, The Physician in Literature, *and* Albert Schweitzer's Mission: Healing and Peace. *He is a trustee of the American Institute of Stress and the Institute for the Advancement of Health. He is a member of the Advisory Board of the Center for Health Communication of Harvard University and the Center for Psychological Studies in the Nuclear Age, an affiliate of Harvard Medical School.*

Mr. Cousins was one of the founders of public television in the United States, serving as Chairman of NET, the predecessor organization to the Corporation for Public Broadcasting. He is the recipient of the United Nations Peace Medal, the American Peace Award, the Albert Schweitzer Award of John Hopkins University, the Walter C. Alvarez Memorial Award for medical writing of the American Medical Writers association of the American Medical Association, the Award of the Government of Canada for service to the environment, the Family of Man Award, the City of Hiroshima Award (for carrying out medical rehabilitation projects for the victims of the bombing), the Personal Medallion of Pope John XXIII for his role in negotiating the release from prison of Josyph Cardinal Slipyi and Joseph Cardinal Beran.

Portraits of Passion: Aging, Defying the Myth

Cousins is president of the World Federalist Association of the United States. He has carried out diplomatic missions abroad as personal emissary for Presidents Eisenhower, Kennedy, and Johnson.

———— ❖ ————

You ask about work. I'm not sure I know what work is. All of my life I've been in the fortunate position of being asked to do something I deeply enjoy. This goes back to my school years when I was the editor of the school paper and extends through my years at the *Saturday Review* and my present connection at the UCLA School of Medicine. Perhaps it has something to do with Toynbey's notion of challenge and response. The challenge was there; the response was almost automatic.

You ask about family influence. I was one of four children. The parental influence was approximately the same for each child, but the effects or responses were quite different. The only similarity perhaps has to do with our literary interests. We all started out in literary careers. I was the editor of the *Saturday Review.* My sister was a book editor at Random House. My brother was the head of the book publishing operation of *Reader's Digest.* So we tended to move in that particular arena, and you might reasonably conclude that a familial influence was at work.

At the Columbia's Teachers College I was very fortunate in being able to get close to John Dewey, William Heard Kilpatrick, and Harold Rugg. One of the things in life of which I'm proudest is that when Kilpatrick and Rugg retired, and were asked to name the one student, out of the many thousands they taught, who would represent the student population at their retirement dinner, they both designated me.

I look back with a great deal of warmth on the association with John Dewey. There were evenings at his home where the students would sit at his feet and ask him about the Russian Revolution, or about Trotsky, or about his own philosophy in life. The Teachers College experience was a very important one, because of the cross-fertilization of ideas it afforded. It wasn't just educational. It had to do with philosophy, history, art, psychology, politics, literature.

Almost everything I experienced or worked at had educational value. The *Saturday Review* was the most profound educational experience of all. I really grew up on the *Saturday Review*. I had mentors: Henry Canby, Amy Loveman, Christopher Morley, William Rose Benet. The entire world of literature burst into flower for me at *Saturday Review*. I was certainly lucky. The nature of the job meant you had to keep educating yourself.

At the UCLA Medical School, I had an idea it would be possible to identify the pathways through which the emotions registered on the brain. Also, to explore the physiological effects of such positive emotions as love, hope, will to live, faith, purpose, determination, and festivity. The medical school encouraged me in this direction. As a result, we have the most comprehensive program of its kind in any medical school. We have been able to mount research that has justified the original hunches.

It's gratifying to receive letters from people who've had good results through our program in confronting their illnesses. It's also gratifying to meet people across the country who say they're alive because they were emboldened to make an extra effort because of our encouragement. I never advocated our approaches as an alternative to traditional medicine, only as an integral part of it.

Looking back, I can see that early experiences play a part in my thinking about health. As a kid I never expected to go very far. I had TB at the age of ten. But I was able to get stronger and better at each chronological plateau in life, I think I'm healthier now at 75 than I was at 25. I discovered life to be more rewarding at each level. So I look forward to the next plateau.

Everything that's happened up to now comes under the heading of good luck. The important thing about life is to stockpile beautiful memories. That's where the proof of life is stored. And that's when you know whether your life has come to anything. I relish future prospects. I enjoy confronting challenges and disproving the experts.

I had a heart attack in 1980. Some of the specialists said that my chances of living out the year without major surgery were unacceptably low. My experience in refuting those glum forecasts has given me confidence in the way the human body works and has bolstered my respect for the human healing system. It also gave me confidence in the way raw determination can be translated into physical strength.

As I say, I've been hounded by good luck all my life. I can't think of anything that is beyond human capability. One of the most important things we've done at UCLA is to share our grants with other medical researchers around the country who are also interested in mind-body interactions.

I've been blessed with a remarkable wife, far beyond anything I deserved. She is central in my life. She is a can-do person, and takes great satisfaction in smoothing the way for me. I've never heard a whine out of her in 51 years, although she has heard a few from me.

At this age, you begin to get the dividends of all the investments you've made - and I'm not referring to stocks and bonds. You enter into a sort of a harvesting period. I know I've done more writing in the last ten years than I've ever done before. True, there are still dragons to slay in the world, there are still mountains to climb. I have a pretty good sense of my own inadequacies. I procrastinate, the enjoyment of living gets in the way of things I ought to be doing. I don't feel guilty about fun I'm having in life.

Old age is an arbitrary concept, conceived and imposed by society, but deeply flawed biologically. It fosters a numbers game by which individuals are condemned biologically. Things are supposed to happen when you arrive at a certain number, whether it's 50, 65, 75 and people tend to move down the path of their expectations. It seems to me that the acceptance of these numbers acts as a hex, and represents the principle problem of aging. You have a notion of other people you've seen at that age, people with infirmities and limitations, and you tend to invite those limitations. The notion of decay and degeneration has to be as much psychological as it is biological. We have to avoid the semantics of defeat.

For example, you may go to a rheumatologist at the age of 50-55 and say, "I can't seem to turn my neck very well", or "I have trouble in my hips". They will tell you that you're suffering from a degenerative condition. The word degenerative seems to rule out reversal. I can think of nothing more important than to defy the semantics.

I remember having a meeting in '67 or '68 with a rheumatologist who noticed I had some difficulty in turning my neck. He manipulated my neck with his hands, asked me to turn left and right, and then dumped on me the semantics of catastrophe. He told me I had to get used to the fact that I had a degenerative condition. With each passing year, however, I was able to turn my neck more and more. Now I have a full turning radius. When I had a heart attack, I was told I had to cut back sharply in life and give up strenuous sports. That was 10 years ago; now I play tennis and golf. My hunch is that I am healthy not despite the exercise but because of it.

Why some people age well and others do not is a complicated equation. The main factors include genetics, general health, outlook on life, nutrition, and a strong sense of purpose. These factors vary with the individual, to be sure. The part played by free will is large and all too often is denied or minimized.

It helps to have a lot of unfinished business on your hands. There's a play on King Charles I want to write; I'm also finishing a very large historical novel. There's a great deal of research I want to undertake at UCLA on the physiological effects of positive emotions. I must not overlook the importance of fun. It's fun to be able to refute negative predictions, whether by tax experts or health experts or anyone who makes flat statements about what can't be done. I think back on a project to bring some thirty Japanese young ladies who had been disfigured by the atomic bombing to the United States for medical and surgical care. Cultural anthropologists consulted by the State Department flatly opposed the project, predicting that it would fail because of the cultural gap between the two countries. It would be too difficult, the experts said, for the girls to adjust, nor could they sustain the strange situation in American hospitals. What the experts underestimated was the bridging power of the outstretched hand. Also the power of loving relationships.

It's always important to consult the experts, certainly; it's even more important to follow your own convictions. There's no harm in going to the experts, but don't hesitate to make up your own mind.

Editor's Note: Norman Cousins passed away in November 1990.

PART FOUR

The Search For Personal Fulfillment

Steve Allen

CHAPTER TWENTY

Steve Allen

The best way to describe Steve Allen and his work is a quote by singer Andy Williams, "Steve Allen does so many things, he's the only man I know who's listed on every one of the Yellow Pages." He still appears frequently on television as a comedian, and has worked steadily in that medium since the 1950's. He created The Tonight Show, *has authored 35 published books, and continues to produce an outpouring of novels, plays, musical comedies, poems, magazine and newspaper articles. He starred on Broadway in the* Pink Elephant; *and has appeared in several motion pictures, including* The Benny Goodman Story.

Although he is best known as a comedian, Steve Allen's primary gift is for the composition of music. For more than 35 years he has enjoyed a career as a composer, lyricist, conductor, singer, and pianist. He is in the Guinness Book of World Records *as the most prolific composer of modern times. To date, he has written over 4000 songs.*

He has written the score for several musicals, including the Broadway production of Sophie *and the CBS-TV version of* Alice in Wonderland. *His dramatic play,* The Wake, *garnered an L.A. Drama Critics' nomination as best play of 1977. He starred in the critically-acclaimed NBC series* The Steve Allen Comedy Hour, *and created, wrote, and hosted the award-winning PBS-TV series* Meeting of Minds. *He has been inducted into the TV Academy's Hall of Fame.*

Mr. Allen was born in New York on December 26, 1921, and is married to actress-comedienne Jayne Meadows.

———❖———

Portraits of Passion: Aging, Defying the Myth

There is a pleasure in work. I think it's naive or ignorant to assume that people work because it's the only way they can arrange to get clothes on their back, food on their table, and a roof over their heads. That is almost certainly true of some jobs. Much of the work in the world is either demeaning, physically tiresome or monotonous. But those of us who work in the creative professions are very fortunate.

I don't know of any of us who started our work because it looked profitable. The painters paint because they found out they could and they love it. Same thing goes for the sculptors, the poets, or the actors. It is just fun. George Burns is a multi-millionaire. He's now, I think, 427 years old and still out there performing constantly and well. Bob Hope is, I think, 157, something close to that. He has more money than God, and is constantly working. It can't be because he needs the money. He just has fun in front of audiences.

I have tried other jobs and I did not enjoy them. So I didn't do them long. I worked one summer, as a very young fellow, in a clothing store in Chicago, as a salesman. I was the worst salesman at the Washington Shirt Company of downtown Chicago. So what sense would it've made for me to say, "No, by golly, I've got to lick this thing." Today I'd still be selling clothes someplace.

I did not have parents that were supportive of my creative interests. I recommend that parents do get into the act by encouraging in supportive ways, which is obviously superior to their doing the opposite. To say, "Your poems are lousy, Bobby. Get a job as an insurance salesman." or whatever, is a terrible thing to do, even if Bobby's poems *are* lousy. They ought to find some very delicate way to bring that to his attention but not deliberately discourage him.

A great part of my creativity must have a genetic explanation. My mother was once described by Milton Berle as the funniest woman in vaudeville. And as funny as she was on stage, she was even funnier off. She just had the gift of being able to make others laugh. My father did a little singing and dancing, but whatever abilities I have to make others feel amused is, I assume, somehow connected to my mother's genetic equipment.

In childhood I got laughs on the street with my friends, but I never tried to make my mother laugh. I never tried to make my aunts or uncles laugh. In fact, one of their nicknames for me around the house was The Sphinx, meaning that I hardly ever opened my mouth. But I was encouraged by two teachers to such an extent that I later dedicated two of my books to them. One was a public school teacher, the other was in a Catholic parochial school.

The latter was Sister Mary Sarathia, and there's nothing particularly magical or remarkable about what she did for me. She simply took an interest in me. And that was 98% of it, right there. I wasn't getting much encouragement of that sort in the home. She discovered in me the ability to write and she gave me writing assignments and congratulated me on my essays and poems and little plays. The same thing happened again when I attended Hyde Park High School in Chicago. A teacher named Marguerite Byrne found out I could write and she put me on the staff of the school magazine and made me, I think, poetry editor. She encouraged me to enter essay contests and to submit poetry to newspapers. So, that's a good thing, but it cannot explain the ability to write a good poem in the first place.

The first person whose work I became emotionally attached to, although I never met the gentleman, in my capacity as both funny person and professional writer, was Robert Benchley. He was, as you know, one of the great American humorists of the 1930's and 40's. He was originally a journalist and wrote funny things for newspapers and even funnier speeches. I first found out about him by wandering through second-hand bookstores. Even as a child, I was fascinated by bookstores.

It's obvious that there are different kinds of payoffs. The payoff is immediate for the entertainer, whether he's a trombone player, a comedian, actor, whatever, at least if he addresses audiences. The audiences give you an immediate rating. You can be in very little doubt as to how well or how poorly you're doing. If you do funny things, you get a lot of laughter. Those are ego-reinforcing and I suppose that must have something to do with why Bob Hope, Red Skelton, Milton Berle, and other now quite old entertainers are still out there doing their marvelous work. It is just sheer fun. I think the average person can understand that easily.

I argued, in one of my books a few years ago called *How to be Funny,* that's because everybody is funny, everyone's had the experience of repeating a joke that their barber told them yesterday or thinking of a little witticism to say at a dinner party. We all like that moment when everyone else in the room laughs. It's 14 seconds of wonderful ego reward.

I recall an instance long ago in the late 1940's, when I was going through a great deal of emotional and personal turmoil. My first marriage was falling apart. It was about as bad a time emotionally as I've ever suffered. Nevertheless five nights a week I had to go on the air for an hour and do a comedy show, ad lib.

During that hour I felt fine. I had no problems. First, I was busy. The audience showed up because they were fans. So I had 300 people reacting and screaming and laughing. I was the happiest man on Earth for that 60 minutes every night. But as soon as I said thank you and goodnight, then life was a total loss to me again. I was back to the painful realities.

Since I travel a lot, I am finding at the age of sixty-eight that my suitcases are considerably heavier than I found them 20 years ago, and sometimes the steps are a little higher and so forth. But except for surgery for cancer, fortunately totally successful surgery, about six years ago, my health much of my life has been quite good. And I've always been a bit athletic. I'm not a jock type, I've been too busy for that, but I work out, I exercise.

But there was one hurdle. At the age of forty I did feel the click of the big wheel of time. I didn't get depressed by it or start drinking, but I remember thinking, wow, forty. Forty did bring itself to my attention. Oddly enough, I sailed past fifty. It didn't mean a damn. I don't know why. You'd think there would be more worries, but it didn't worry me at all.

Oddly enough I became much more productive after that. There's a lesson in that. As regards writing generally, I don't think I did anything worth noting before thirty. Most of my short stories were rejected by editors and publishers, and rightly so. Only a few of my poems were that good, most of them were lightweight. I've since had two volumes of poetry published and I have a third ready to go, so I continue to write. But my point is I'm writing much better poetry, and better songs, in my sixties than I did as a young fellow. My novels, short stories, the more serious forms of literature that I produce, have seen nothing but a process of improvement. If you do any task, whether it's hitting a ping pong ball or writing an opera, whatever you do you would tend to do it better the more you do it.

I've never been an easily discouraged person. I have my periods of depression, low energy or feelings of negativity, but they're always short. I remember something I wrote when I was about seventeen. The point was that no matter how depressed you are today, you can be absolutely assured that before the passage of very much time you will feel a good deal better. I had already been through that thing myself 200 times at that early age.

We are all products of our social environment. My own background is lower-middle class Chicago Irish Catholic. It had both positives and negatives to it. One of the negatives, for example, was rampant anti-Semitism. It was never of the what you might call prejudice of the Hitlerian or European sort. It was never that virulent. It was more stupid. It had to do with what neighborhood you grew up in, who beat up your little brother. But anyway, that was one of the negatives of that culture. My personal philosophy now is a mixture of Christian and humanist elements. I think every individual, even though he calls himself a Baptist, a Jew, a Catholic, a Muslim, really has his own religion.

In show business there is a certain amount of bias about the factor of age. I've already mentioned some gifted entertainers who although very old are still active. There is no concern about my appearance, anymore than there is about Bob Hope's or George Burns' appearance. So if you do comedy, you're much better off. It's the straight actors who are in trouble as they get older, unless they're awfully good actors such as Art Carney. In accepting his Academy Award, Carney said, "and I'd like to thank my agent, who said to me, take the part, you are old". He got a scream from both the young people and the old people in the audience who understood it even more. So, good actors, talented people like Art, can continue to be employed, but they don't play romantic leads anymore.

As a professional, there's a certain respect you get for nothing more than survival. You just get a different respect from audiences. The first time I ran into that I was a member of an audience that was reacting in that way. This was back about 1941, I was just a kid wandering around Hollywood. Anyway, somebody on the sidewalk gave me a ticket to a radio show and I had nothing to do so I went into the studio. The announcer came out and said, "blah, blah, blah, Bob Hope" and Bob walked out. He got about four minutes of applause just for being there. And I was one of the people applauding. I realized that Bob had been part of our childhood, our growing up. He was very important on radio in the early 30's. He had made movies with Bing Crosby. He had his own weekly comedy show on radio, so he was just as big a star then as he is now. We were giving him that kind of affectionate respect for still being around, just for showing up. So anyway, on a less dramatic level, for the last 15 years of my experience, I now get a different sort of reaction from audiences, just by walking out on stage.

Work keeps you young. Some people are thrilled with their retirement. They're smart enough to keep reading, going to plays, they have good friends and they have a lot of fun. It also helps if they have the money to have fun. But I would say even in that case, even if you're a millionaire and you never have to lift your finger again I would still say, work. If you don't have a job, go offer your services to the Red Cross, offer your services to the mental health group in your town. Otherwise you'll sit there like an idiot in front of the television all day long. So work, work, work right up until you drop. That is one of my prescriptions.

Am I proud of my gifts? No. Possibly because of my early philosophical conditioning, I have problems with pride. Whenever one of my four sons does something marvelous, somebody might say to me, I'll bet you're proud of them. And I say, you're damned right I am. But that kind of pride is okay because it has nothing to do with me. But when people say you must be very proud of yourself, no, I would be proud if I somehow had created something out of nothing, but I didn't. I was simply able to do something. So I'm very grateful to God, the accidents of nature, genetics, whatever it is that explains my abilities. But I had nothing to do with it, so why should I be proud?

I thank my secretary, Pat Quinn, and my wife for keeping sane and sensible environments around me. With regards to our home, Jayne does many of the things that in most homes the man does. If a lamp breaks, she calls up the lamp shop or she calls a man in to fix it. I'm not saying I refuse to do it. She's just gifted at that and I'm not. I'm gifted at 12 other things, all of which help to keep us alive and well.

Also I love and I support her. We travel together sometimes, work together. I'm fortunate in dozens of ways that she is there for me in that regard. Jayne is very knowledgeable about comedy. She performs it well, for one thing. And she's a great editor, with very good judgement. She's right 98% of the time, if she thinks a sketch or a performance funny. Nobody rates 100%. I solicit her advice even when I don't think she's very happy about giving it. She has a good sense of humor. She's not a joke-oriented person, but she understands them. It's interesting in that specific connection that our son Bill, although he himself is not a jokester or humorist, is in charge of comedy development at the MTM studios, because he grew up around the business with a funny mother and father, and then hung out with writers. He really does understand the business. We were always very supportive of him and he's deserved it.

Gifts need to be encouraged. In my book, *Dumbth and 81 Ways to Make Americans Smarter,* I referred to Charles Kettering, the famous inventor. He was a perfect case of a gifted child who had the good fortune to come to the attention of teachers who recognized his unique ability. There always has to be, even in the case of such obviously genetically superior individuals, either some luck or accident. You meet a teacher who recognizes your potential and encourages it, or there's a family member who knows that you're very superior with whatever your gift might be.

Annabelle Palkes Godwin

CHAPTER TWENTY-ONE

Annabelle Palkes Godwin

Annabelle Godwin was born in St.Louis, Missouri, on December 23rd, 1920. In 1945 she received her B.S. degree from Washington University of St. Louis in Education and Drama. She received her M.A. in 1967 in Early Childhood Education from the University of California at Los Angeles. She has three children and two grandchildren.

Mrs. Godwin opened and directed the Burbank Temple Emanuel Nursery School in 1959. In 1967 she started and directed Temple Beth Hillel Nursery School. She began to teach for the Los Angeles Community College District in 1968, and later that year at U.C.L.A. Extension in Child Development. She is now a Full Professor at Los Angeles Mission College.

She has been an active member of the National Association for the Education of Young Children, a Founding Member and Past President of the Association for Early Jewish Education. She serves on the Board of the California Children's Lobby, which she represents on the Los Angeles Mayor's Advisory Committee on Child Care.

Godwin produced a educational film in 1975, Creative Experiences with Body Movement, *and in 1988 co-chaired a committee that compiled a book entitled* Setting Up for Infant Care for NAEYC.

❖

I love what I do and I am happy that I'm in a situation where I can continue to work and age has not been an issue. I am very fortunate that I have my health and lots of energy. I'm overwhelmed with the appreciation my students give me for what I do for them. That's marvelous.

My parents both came from Europe. My father spoke seven or eight languages, and he worked at Ellis Island as an interpreter. He was college educated, which at that time was rare. My mother went to school only until the fourth grade. Education was tremendously important to my mother and to my father. They struggled through the Depression. I was the youngest child. My brothers and sisters were given music lessons on various instruments, but when I came along there wasn't money for that kind of thing.

My mother worked hard at home. She altered clothes and took in roomers. When my father lost his business, my brother and sister went to work to help the family. I was little and that wasn't expected of me. Things had begun to recover by the time I finished high school. My parents allowed me a lot of freedom. I was interested in dramatics and I was given free lessons. My mother was particularly proud of my performing and I had a wonderful teacher.

I continued my activity in Drama in high school and college where it was my major. The only way I could get a degree in Drama was to also take Education. I really feel that in many ways what I learned in Drama classes was very helpful to me as a teacher. In a college classroom you speak before an audience. I feel that it all came together for me, and I'm still performing, but with different material.

My mother was one of my early mentors. She insisted, when I didn't get a scholarship, she would help to support me through college. A number of my teachers encouraged me all along the way. My Drama teacher, Thelma Smith, was simply marvelous to me, giving me lessons free of charge. In high school the teacher who sponsored the newspaper was a mentor to me. I became editor of the school newspaper. The head of the Drama Club, Miss Malone, was another mentor, as was my Drama professor, Alfred O. Wilkinson, at Washington University.

There was a room I used to go into in high school. It was actually the Drama room and much of the time no one would be in there, so I could go there and be alone. I used to call that the crying room -- a place to go when I was upset. I discovered something when I was there. I reasoned that life goes in cycles, and for me it has always worked out that way. Things go up and down. I know that there are times when things are going just marvelously and everything seems to work out. I also know that there will be times when my desires will not be fulfilled.

The other thing I learned is I can't control other people. I can only influence them. I can only control myself. I can only try to influence those who are closest to me. I learned it early and I think I'm better for it.

My philosophical base comes from my father. He once said, "You live your life the best you can without hurting other people." I think of the play, *The Time of Your Life*, because that was that kind of statement. I think it also comes from Biblical truth: treat others as you would have others treat you. I think that has been a basic tenet of my life.

I've been very lucky. I have a very supportive husband. I could not have done what I did without that support. I worked in a field that paid very little and was fortunate to have someone to support me financially. He also supported me emotionally.

I want to do something to make things better for people, particularly children. One of the things that my daughter, Sara, said to me was, "Mother, don't ever quit work, don't ever retire." I said, "When your health gives way you don't have a lot of choices, as is the case with many people."

When I get an idea I want to see it come to fruition. I am taking a sabbatical to study various infant/toddler programs, especially in the San Fernando Valley where I teach. I recently visited Canada where they have good child care programs. They have a different attitude towards children -- they care about young children. This country does not do well by young children at all -- we'd much rather put money into jails and the military.

I think why some people age well and other do not depends on their attitude towards life. Part of it is, where you choose to be involved. I like being involved, planning and getting things done -- enjoy people and doing.

What I have sometimes said should be written on my epitaph is, "if I said I would do it, you can count on it."

I guess I have enthusiasm for life.

Ann Brebner

CHAPTER TWENTY-TWO

Ann Brebner

Ann was born in New Zealand. In 1946, she graduated from the University of New Zealand with an AB degree in Abnormal Psychology. From 1946 to 1952 she was the head of the English Department of Craighead Diocesan School, as well as a part-time associate therapist.

Ann was accepted at the Old Vic Theatre School in London in 1952, as a student director. From 1957-60 she was on the faculty of Dominican College, and in addition to her teaching produced two major performances a year. She has lectured extensively to college and professional audiences, and was one of the co-founders of the Marin County Shakespeare Company in California.

Ms. Brebner established Brebner Agencies, Inc. in 1960, representing actors for motion pictures, television and commercials. In 1983, she was honored by over 400 members of the motion picture and entertainment industry, with George Lucas being one of the speakers. In 1984, Ms. Brebner was the casting director for the films Massive Retaliation, *and* Smooth Talk; *and co-authored screenplays for* Dearly Beloved, Going Home, *and* The Anniversary.

Her book, Setting the Actor Free: Overcoming the Creative Blocks, *was published in 1990.*

---------- ❖ ----------

I feel so much better when I work than when I don't. That is personal fulfillment, feeling good, my mind being so busy that's it's difficult to turn it off to go to sleep. When I wake up in the morning it's wonderful, even if the day were 48 hours long I wouldn't get done what I want to do. I love feeling like that.

I think that even at this point in my life, there's still a little edge of parental influence about the work ethic. My mother died at my birth and I was an only child. I think my father wanted a son, so he taught me to be completely independent. In an odd kind of way, I grew up without the feminine. I grew up like a boy in some ways, even though my great aunt looked after me until I was 12. I could take a boat out on a lake by myself when I was very young. I knew all the parts of an automobile engine, I could shoot a rabbit, I could skin a rabbit, I could clean a fish.

The other side of that coin is when I first went to a girls' school, I felt that I didn't fit in, in a major way. I had had no mother to say to me, nice little girls don't do this. My female-figure was a generation removed, so the things my great-aunt taught me were equally likely to be out of date, not wrong, but dated. And sometimes laughable to one's peers when one is 6, 7, 8, 9.

My father was very, very undemonstrative emotionally, and he was extremely demanding. His idea of my over-achieving, however, was to be a doctor, and for some reason he wanted me to be an anesthesiologist. I don't know why. If I had gone into the medical profession I wanted to be a psychiatrist. The shadow figure through all of that is the mother who wasn't there. For a long, long time I felt that you don't miss what you don't have. Then in the course of therapy, bingo, you know, you invent what you don't have, which is far more powerful in some ways than the real thing. You can invent an image that in a sense is perfection. So you strive mightily for that.

When I was in my early 40's I was divorced, and subsequently bought a house. I was giving a Christmas party. I came downstairs and lit the fire, lit the candles. I was walking around the house. I thought, I'm showing this to someone. I sat down on the front stairs and realized that I was showing it to my mother. I was saying, is this enough? Is this beautiful enough? Is this expensive enough? Have I succeeded yet? Will you acknowledge me in some way, please? I felt, no, she won't. You'd better start doing things for yourself. That was a major change for me.

I've really changed much of the way I think, much of the way I live, certainly my process of choosing what to do. In the last 10 years that has changed radically, I really don't do anything I don't want to do. I am almost totally unconscious of what I've achieved in the past. I really do work in the moment. People will say to me, what are you working so hard for? You know how to do this. You've done it before. But every project still feels exciting and adventurous to me.

My suspicion is my mother would have approved of what I do, partly because of her love of music and her creativity, I gather, her extraordinary creativity. My uncle, my mother's brother, absolutely approved of me. He was the one person who said to go for it when I wanted to become a concert pianist. He would sit down at night after he came in off the ranch and say, play for me. He was the only person who ever asked that in that loving way.

Michel Saint Denis, who was head of the Old Vic School, was very influential in my later development. Michel's curiosity is what he gave me, a respect for the 'not knowingness', the waiting for the creative solution, staying in indecision long enough to know. That stayed with me. I can remember him saying, "what is the truth, dear chap?" then waiting till I got it, and never moving away until my curiosity made me discover it. That's the gift he gave me.

On one level, in my profession, there is a sense of belonging, a sense of having the family I never had, especially in theatre and film. I'm very aware of that, and you bond to those people very quickly. You sort of step over the 'getting to know' and you're just bonded in a creative pursuit. Every production, every film, every stage play I've directed or been in, you get a new family. They're all dependent on your success and devoted to that, not devoted to criticism and failure. So that is part of it for me. Part of it is that wonderful, juicy, almost sexual feeling of struggle for creative accomplishment. It's very akin to sexual energy. It's very seductive, a bonding with people and with yourself in your own internal creative vision. It's a release, and it's a celebration, and it's a lot of things that I don't know any other way to get.

I had always feared that I would die at the same age as my mother, so I was astounded to find myself at 37 with a baby and alive. It was like a whole new life. It was really a rebirth. Three and a half years ago my oldest son's lover died of AIDS. That's a such a strange experience. You don't expect your children's mates to die while you're alive. Life has become more precious to me now. I look at the number of people in my profession who are dying. I say to myself, "you'd better not screw around and waste time."

In Milan Kundera's book, *Life is Elsewhere*, there's a wonderful statement, "Reality does not discuss, reality simply is." I add to that, you better see it, if you see reality clearly, I think it makes you very free. If you try and change reality, you're going to bang against one wall after another and become frustrated.

The older I get the more I believe in the internal. It's all inside, rather than out there, understanding and knowing all of the trauma or joy or whatever it is that one has experienced. At the same time, I believe that there is a force of some kind that is greater than I can conceive of. I also believe quite firmly that it is inappropriate to want to understand it.

Some of the most intimate relationships I've had were with people who were much younger. It doesn't mean I don't have a lot of friends of my own general age group. I tend to be internally exactly the age of who I'm talking to, not in behavior necessarily but internally. I don't know what that is, but there's no barrier.

I was talking to a man who's about 39 the other day. It was after the Gorbachev speech at Stanford. He said, this is the first night of my life that I have not been afraid. It was such a revelation to me about the fear of that generation, how powerful it has been. We went on talking for hours about fear. There was absolutely nothing separating us at all. You can eliminate the shroud of age and get to the real person.

I used to feel busy, striving, getting, accumulating, I've got to do this, I've got to do that, not centered, not grounded, looking outside me for what in the hell life was. I know now not to do that. So I select what I want to do in a very different way. There's very little of my life that I don't absolutely enjoy. Very little. The minute I get disenchanted, I think, whoops, wait a minute, how did you get into this and why are you doing it? The discomfort level used to mean, try harder, get through it, do this, do it successfully. That's all training. Now, if it's uncomfortable, or if the discomfort level becomes evident, I think, wait a minute now, just stop and look at this. Do you really want to do this?

I have wondered whether aging well has something to do with having found and being able to actualize one's dream. I have a feeling that people who either don't find their dream, or are unable to walk on that path, somewhere along the line lose hope, or self-esteem. If you don't have hope, you die. That's the one element the human organism has to have.

I know what my dream is and there's no way I can get it finished. I think that's what certainly gives me the juice. If I didn't have the dream, oh my god, how would I get up in the morning? I have an ability to know what I can do and what I can't. I've always been able to say, I know how to do that, and do it. I've looked at other things and thought, how the hell do you do that?

I've felt for a long time that I'm weaving a tapestry for which there is no design, and it has never been woven before, and it will never be woven again. So I must weave, even though I may not be able to see where it fits right now, I will see it next year, the year after, ten years from now. I'll see why that color of thread got woven at that point. Although what I may have wished for was another color right then.

David Steinberg

CHAPTER TWENTY-THREE

David Steinberg

David Steinberg was born on November 15th, 1913 in Newark, New Jersey. He went to Lehigh University in Bethlehem, Pennsylvania, where in addition to receiving a degree in Fine Arts, he edited the college humor magazine. He presently writes a column for the San Francisco Examiner *called "Seniorities" and in 1985 he originated the San Francisco State University course entitled,* Debunking Myths About Aging in America, *taught as part of the S.F.S.U.'s Applied Gerontology Certificate Program. He has worked as a theatre editor and as a New York theatrical publicist.*

In 1989, he was recognized as the California Aging Network's Media Advocate of the Year. *Steinberg is an active campaigner to eliminate the term "senior citizen," which he believes has negative connotations that lead people over 65 to talk themselves into premature decrepitude. One of David Steinberg's favorite saying is, "I used to help grandmothers across the street -- now I follow them."*

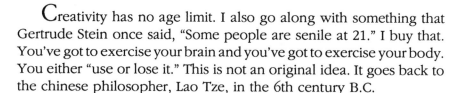

Creativity has no age limit. I also go along with something that Gertrude Stein once said, "Some people are senile at 21." I buy that. You've got to exercise your brain and you've got to exercise your body. You either "use or lose it." This is not an original idea. It goes back to the chinese philosopher, Lao Tze, in the 6th century B.C.

I have a cousin who's an 83 year old commercial artist. Like many commercial artists, there was this fine artist waiting to emerge, and be discovered. He has some theories on painting that were novel, which he wanted to experiment with. I found that he and my oldest brother

155

were two of the brightest humans I have ever known. They were omnivorous readers. They knew so much and were interested in everything. I've always looked up to them.

I used to be a newspaperman. When I moved to California I read articles in the newspaper about older persons, written by younger reporters, that annoyed me. They seemed to be in awe of someone as old as their parents who could do anything, or could still function. They seemed to have a notion that at a predetermined age things stopped, inferring individuals achieve instantaneous decrepitude on a specific birthday. This was utter nonsense. That's what prompted me to write a column showing that people, regardless of their age, can love, make love, participate, learn, and do a whole host of things that anyone can do within reason. I thought that somebody should come out and say what had to be said. For that reason, I developed a course of study at San Francisco State on debunking myths about aging in America.

My wife was an extremely creative and intelligent woman. Her illnesses prevented her from achieving her potential. After she died, I decided that whatever creative ability I had or talent I had, I was going to exercise it and write a column about things I felt had to be said about age and society's misconceptions about it. I don't see any reason to stop working because you reach a certain age. In fact, it's important regardless of your age to get up in the morning and have something to do. I think having to meet a deadline, to write a column, is very important. I don't think that chronological age has to do with anything. People have to live and acquire knowledge before they know what it is that they want to do. Their experiences might enable them to make a choice that they couldn't make when they were younger. I say to my readers, explore your psyche, don't give up. Let's do it!

I'm constantly amazed to find that there are many younger people who are reading my column. I get letters and phone calls from them. Also there's a greater reader awareness as the population ages. We are seeing more and more older persons going back to college, learning new things, changing careers, and achieving the dream. I think that the American Dream is not exclusively for younger people. I'm encouraged to see more and more older people accomplishing, doing, and performing. I call this the "postponed dream."

I'm inspired by the older men and women I write about in my column. The 63-year-old woman who became a sex therapist and 10 years later is a marriage counselor. The man who hadn't played tennis for nearly 40 years, started again after back surgery and won championships for 75-year olds on clay, grass and indoor courts. The 60 year-old woman who became a professional actress after raising four children. Fred Ramstedt, over 80, who expects his book of aphorisms to be published soon. That's what inspired me to continue writing my column and feature stories. These people who remain intellectually curious, enterprising, and courageous; they're my inspiration.

In a sense I am experiencing the postponed dream. There are books and critical things that I have to write, and the problem I have is that there are not enough hours in the day. I think that anybody with any feeling has to have some kind of romantic ideas about themselves, about life. Without it, you've got white bread without the crust.

There are individuals who I have admired and respected, but I do not try to emulate anyone. One of my intellectual heroes was Lewis Mumford, who died at the age of 93. Without a university degree he became a college professor. He opened up a whole new idea about urban aesthetics. I'd say Lewis Mumford was our first urban philosopher. He wrote about the culture of cities, and some say he was the first important American environmentalist. The man had lot of universal depth and feeling. He used to write and criticize architecture and write criticism for the *New Yorker*. He wrote *Techniques and Civilization*, a master work. He was a man who I have always admired.

Another person I respected and admired was Andre Malraux, a scholar and activist. He wrote a definitive book on art, *The Voices of Silence*, and a great novel, *Man's Fate*. He fought in the French underground against the Nazis. He later became De Gaulle's Minister of Culture, restored works at the Louvre and permitted American museum patrons to see the great French art in traveling shows here.

I see a deterioration of language that bothers me. I think the English language is a magnificent instrument, and I see it being brutalized, sullied. In fact I think that sometimes I ought to write an article about the need for some new profanity. Even profanity seems to have lost whatever it was supposed to convey. I also see acceptance of many so called creative accomplishments that I think are less than valuable. In other words, I'm not going to make comparisons between music with which I grew up and the current rock music, things like that. However I feel that whatever is good will endure, and those artists in whatever mediums who are solid and good will endure.

Portraits of Passion: Aging, Defying the Myth

The French Chef, Brillat Savarin said, "You are what you eat." I suppose in our society, you are what you do: whether we do jobs or work at things we choose, or whether they're things we fall into. Some people work at things that help them pay the rent or buy groceries. Some want to do more than that. They want to do things that satisfied their soul as well. There are many instances where one will merely work at one job in order to earn the wherewithal they need, but then pursue what they really wanted to pursue.

I see life and aging as a continuum, not an abrupt change from one to the other, but within that continuum you change or shift. The hopeful idea is that you improve, you get better, deeper. Bishop Cumberland, who I have often quoted in my column, says that "You are much more likely to rust out than you are to wear out." I think that this is an abiding philosophy that I have, that you have to do. You have to participate. I write about people who do, and elders who do. The idea of being a participant, not merely a recipient is what's important, no matter how old or young you may be.

John Wooden

CHAPTER TWENTY-FOUR

John Wooden

John Wooden was born in Hall, Indiana in 1910. As head basketball coach for UCLA, he led the Bruins to 10 national championships in 12 seasons before retiring in 1975. He is the only person to be inducted into the Hall of Fame as both a player and coach. He was a three time All-American at Purdue, and National College Player of the Year in 1932.

Among his many honors are: 1964 California Father of the Year; between the years 1964 and 1973 he was voted Coach of the Year six times; in 1970, Sporting News *named him "Sportsman of the Year"; he was* Sports Illustrated's *"Sportsman of the Year." in 1973; in 1974 He received the first James A. Naismith "Peach Basket" Award. He has written two books:* Practical Modern Basketball, *and* They Call Me Coach, *and is currently writing two more. He has also lectured at many coaching clinics throughout the world, and has served as a commentator on nationally televised basketball games for several years. He has been called the greatest coach in college basketball history.*[14]

I think one needs to be involved in something all the time. When you're in a position where you're not involved, where you're not giving in some way, you're through and not really living. You can give in many different ways and need to, or you come to the feeling that you're not needed, which means you have no purpose for which to live.

I enjoy what I'm doing as I like to interact with people. I've always loved to work with young people, and especially with others who are

161

Portraits of Passion: Aging, Defying the Myth

interested in the same things in which I am. Perhaps I can better relate to young people because of the experience I have had with youngsters through the years. It has always been my conviction that one must keep busy. Keeping active with something I enjoy and having time to be with my children, grandchildren, and great-grandchildren, are my reasons for living, now particularly, since I lost my wife a little over five years ago.

I consider myself a teacher and feel that is what a coach should be. You must follow the four basic laws of learning in teaching the fundamentals of a sport as much or more so than you do in teaching a youngster to diagram a sentence or solve a problem. I have said, and a lot of people take this with a little grain of salt, but I really mean it when I say that there were times when I would much rather be up in the stands when the ball game is played and observe the game from there and see whether I've done much of a job of teaching during the week. You can learn more that way than sitting on the bench during a game. I enjoyed planning and conducting the practices, more so than I ever enjoyed the games. The games are something like an examination.

My father had a great influence on my life and values. I was raised on a small farm with three brothers, one older brother and two younger. We lost the farm in The Depression in the twenties before my two younger brothers were old enough to do very much. My father's ethic was that you should never try to be better than someone else, but you should never cease to try to be the best you could be. Later on I came up with my own definition of success, which is peace of mind attained through self-satisfaction in knowing you made the effort to become the best of which you're capable. You see, you're the only one that can know that. You can fool other people, but you yourself will know.

It's much like character and reputation. Your reputation is what others perceive you to be. Your character is what you are. You're the only one who truly knows that. My father believed there's a time for play after the chores are done, first things first, and he insisted on that. But he always felt there's a time for play. In those days there was little radio and no television. Books were read and that started my love of poetry. He would read poetry to us. I can still remember him reading Longfellow's *Hiawatha* and poems from the early American and English poets.

Other mentors were my grade school principal, Earl Warner, and then later my coach in high school, Glenn Curtis, and Ward "Piggie" Lambert, my coach at Purdue. Lambert was also a doctor in Physics, a man with about as high principles as anyone I've ever known. I think that they all had a tremendous effect on me. Probably the one person that had the most influence in my life was my late wife, Nellie. We were high school sweethearts. She encouraged me to go to college when it was very difficult, with no financial aid and no scholarships or anything of that sort. She was so supportive in the role of a coach's wife, which isn't easy in many ways. Her strength had a tremendous effect on me.

Hardly a day goes by that I do not receive a letter from some youngster, or the parents of a youngster that I've had in my summer basketball camps, or an ex-player that felt I have in some way helped them along the way to be more successful. That makes me feel good. I like to feel that in some way I've helped stimulate things that have helped to make them better people.

I think that anyone that's in a position of supervision or leadership, whatever it might be, has an opportunity to make a difference in the lives of others. I hope that I made a difference on the positive side, on the better side. When I receive confirmation of that by letters or word of mouth or something, it makes me feel good.

I think self-analysis is very difficult. I would say that I accepted things as they came along, and I don't think I ever got carried away about a quest for material things, which I think was helpful, and yet I wanted good things for my family. I did what I could for them, but I think there's so much truth in Lincoln's statement that the worst thing you can do for those you love is the things that they could and should do for themselves. I think I accepted things as they went along, and had no particular concerns about what the future would be. I never worried about a job, I felt that I could always get a job.

The loss of my dear wife affected my life view more than anything else. For a couple of years, I didn't want to do anything at all. I had trouble accepting it. But with friends and family, children, grandchildren, doctors and faith, I think I have gradually accepted it. Not that I don't need her as much as ever, but I've been more accepting toward it. There was a time prior to that, that I think I had some fear of death, but now I have no fear, knowing that is the only possibility that I have to be with her again. That's made a change in my outlook. Then the coming along of our great-grandchildren, of whom we now have five, has been of great help.

Portraits of Passion: Aging, Defying the Myth

My philosophical base throughout the years has been a combination of things, no one individual thing. Certain things have made an impression on me. When I first started teaching I read something in an NEA journal that went something like this: "No written word, no spoken plea can teach our youth what they should be. Nor all the books on all the shelves, it's what the teachers are themselves." You need to set a good example for those you are going to teach. As Wilferd Peterson says, you shouldn't be behind with a whip saying "get going", you've got to lead. You've got to be out in front and say, "Follow me, we're in this together. You're not for me, you're with me."

In the position of leadership, there are things you have to do that aren't pleasant, but you have to have certain principles on which you stand, things you believe in. You can't have some for one and some for the other. Although I've always said that you don't treat everybody alike, you try to give each one the treatment they deserve. At one time I had a number of rules and a few suggestions, as time went by I had fewer rules and more suggestions. But there are certain rules I've had that I've stuck with, and it didn't make a difference who it was, whether it was a star player or whether it was someone who might not get to play too much.

You must not let your personal likes and dislikes affect your judgment in trying to develop the team in this sense. If you were in business and trying to make it successful, you must recognize and acknowledge all who are contributing even though you may not like them personally. Of course, they must delegate personal effort to the success of the team. Both you and they must understand that. Alonzo Stagg said, "I never had a player in all my years of coaching that I didn't love. I had some I didn't like and didn't respect, but I loved them just the same."

I think the reason some people age well and others do not is their inability to accept the fact that they're not all powerful. Lincoln said, "Things work out best for those who make the best of the way things work out." Lincoln is my favorite American. He had a wonderful ability to say so many things that were so deep and meaningful in just a few words. I've known a lot of people who could talk forever and not say anything.

The trait of which I am most proud is being at peace with myself. When Socrates was imprisoned, facing imminent and unjust death, the jailers at that particular time were maybe the toughest, meanest people of that era, but couldn't understand his complete serenity as he was facing this unjust and imminent death. They asked him, "Why aren't you preparing for death?" And he said, "I've been preparing for it all my life." That's what we should do. Knowing that you're imperfect and you'll make a lot of mistakes along the way, but just trying to do the best that you can do, and not getting lost in yourself or in material things. When you get things out of perspective, you expect too much, and then I think's when you run into trouble. Never permit excessive jubilation over the joy that comes your way nor excessive dejection over your misfortunes, as for every peak there will be a valley.

Wilson Riles

CHAPTER TWENTY-FIVE

Wilson Riles

Wilson Riles began his career in education as a teacher in a one-room school on an Apache Indian reservation near Pistol Creek, Arizona. He moved to California and joined the State Department of Education in 1958. In 1965, he became Director of Compensatory Education; Deputy Superintendent for Programs and Legislation in 1969; and from 1971 to 1982 he served as the Superintendent of Public Instruction for the State of California. During the same period, he provided leadership in the development of early childhood education programs, special education, educational programs for the gifted and talented, programs for limited and non-english speaking children, and general programs designed to improve education for all students.

Riles earned national recognition during his service as State Superintendent. He has served as President of the Council of State School Officers and has been an advisor to four presidents on national education issues.

Riles received both his Bachelor of Arts and Masters from Northern Arizona University and is a holder of nine honorary doctorates. He is also the recipient of numerous awards for public service and educational leadership.

Wilson Riles is currently President of Wilson Riles and Associates, Inc., an educational consultation firm with headquarters in Sacramento, California.

The enjoyable thing about this stage in my career is that I can make choices. I've been doing my own business and doing my own thing, so to speak, and that is much more relaxing than if I had someone else's schedule. To me it is a change for the better. I don't have the pressures that I once had. Having worked all my life, being able to continue working and doing the things that I enjoy doing, I feel that what is important is what motivates me.

For example, over the years, being involved in education, I realized that from my background and my beginnings I never would have made it had there not been individuals here and there such as teachers, and principals, who encouraged me even though I was in the backwoods of Louisiana. People said, "Boy, get yourself an education. No one is going to take that away from you." They helped me and encouraged me. I went into education and I guess my motivation was to help other kids along the way. As long as I live I will have a motivation to encourage and help other kids.

I was an only child. My father worked in the turpentine woods. He was a turpentine farmer. My mother was a housewife. And as an only child, I was loved and coddled and people used to say that I was a spoiled kid, jokingly. My mother died when I was nine years old, my father three years later. In those days, in small communities, the people were your friends. There was no formal adoption. Friends of my father and mother took me in and what was their's was mine. I went down to New Orleans and worked my way through McDonogh No. 35 High School. I finished right in the middle of the Depression. Then we moved to Arizona where jobs in the timber industry opened up.

As a boy at 8 or 9, losing your mother, I can't think of a thing as painful as that. As a matter of fact, it took me a couple of years before I could face up to what happened. It seemed to me that, I can't explain this very well because I don't understand it. I either heard it in a dream or a half dream or something. One night I thought that I heard my mother's voice. It had been a couple of years that I had been going through trauma and the voice said to me, "Son, the worst thing that could ever happen to you has already happened." That was a turnaround for me. Then I was willing to face up to whatever else came along. And it so happened that a year later my father died. It was not nearly as traumatic as it was when my mother died. So I have to say that losing my mother at nine years old was the most devastating thing that ever happened, and also the most strengthening.

I've had other problems. Living in the South at that time, the humiliation, the segregation, the unfairness of it were things that we had to learn to deal with. But always there were people that did not believe in that, but were caught up in the same thing. And I was fortunate enough from time to time to meet some of them. As a matter of fact, when I came to Northern Arizona University one of the most difficult things was not knowing what it really was like. I thought all white people had no problems. I thought many of them would be against me. Living in that situation, I thought, my god, white people do have problems and most of them have so many they don't have time to pay any attention to me. Then I began to make some friends, a small circle of friends, and of course I was always skeptical. But we went into some situations which by any count, any evaluation you could make, they were friends. And of course, when I look back on my experience in the South, I didn't love everybody because they were black. These were experiences that led me in the end to view people as individuals and to really understand that there's good, bad, weak, strong, wise, foolish among all of us and that we should not evaluate people on their race.

After going to Northern Arizona University, I knew that I was afraid moving directly out of the South into an all-white situation. As a matter of fact, when I enrolled on the campus, I was the only black student. I had all kinds of fears about what might or might not happen. I was only able to enroll because of the National Youth Administration program that provided money so that you could work on the campus. That's how I got in. But the story that I remember is that there were teachers there that were supportive and guided me along without me really being aware of what they were doing. It was years later when I went back and talked to them that I realized the kinds of things that they were doing that were supportive, and all of these things affected my life and my views and my development.

One name I never will forget is Forrest Paul Augustine, the principal of the elementary school. His saying was, "You can learn, you must learn, and I'll help you." The other thing that he did was he put images before us of people who had problems greater than ours, little stories, people like Booker T. Washington and George Washington Carver. Of course, when you begin to read about their lives and the fact that they didn't give up, those are the kinds of things that impressed me. There was another principal down at New Orleans in those days. This principal was Dr. Lucien Alexis, who by the way had his doctorate degree from Harvard, which was unusual for a black in those days. He was principal of an all-black high school, and I guess he was in that position because that was where he was able to get a job. At any rate, we benefited from that kind of leadership.

I presume that much of what happens to an individual is luck, or you happen to be in the right place at the right time. It's not all that, because you have to take advantage of the opportunities and sometimes make choices, mine has been an opportunity to have increasing responsibilities. Credit must go to my wife, Mary Louise, who was encouraging and when I was ready to make a next step, she was supportive in that. I didn't have the worry of having her discourage me or, on the other hand, push me into a situation. She encouraged my growth, and said, "Look, you go for it."

The only time that my wife dragged her feet on any move that I was anticipating was when I decided to run for the State Superintendent of Public Instructions: a statewide elective office in California. When I decided to do it, she was dragging her feet and so was my youngest son, Phillip. So finally one evening, I said why in the world aren't you supporting me in this endeavor that I'm about to undertake. And my youngest son said, "Because, Daddy, we don't want you to get hurt. And neither mother or I, we don't want you to get hurt." I told him what I had been through in my life. To lose your mother at nine and your father at 12, and to have to work and struggle all the time, it cannot get any worse. I cannot be hurt on that, and I'm willing to take the chance. Their response was okay, if you see it that way you have our support. And of course from then on they were totally supportive.

I never gave much thought to getting older. I got tired of having birthdays, of course. And then when I finished my last term and lost the election, all of a sudden I had to take a look at what I had to do. As a matter of fact, I was offered a job, a number of jobs, but I wanted to do something else. I had always wanted to do some writing, so I decided after 40 years of this education business I should know something that someone else might want to know or need to know and be willing to pay for it. So I decided then one thing I might do is consulting. Some of my friends who had retired had done consulting kind of out of their hip pockets. I didn't want to do that. If I were going to do it, I would put it on a business basis. People began to call for assistance and that's how I got into it.

I didn't run for State Superintendent because I'm black, that was not the issue. I felt I could do the job that needed to be done for all kids.

The fact that I happen to be black was incidental. My dream and hope today is that we recognize that the different ethnic groups are the strength of this country. When you get right down to it, most of your people regardless of background, they want someone with respect and understanding and sensitivity. The politicians, the media, still have a difficult time in understanding that today. They frame most things in color and ethnicity when they should be framing it in what does the individual believe and what would be fair for everybody.

My father and mother were Methodists by religion, and in the African Methodist Episcopal Church. This was just the Christian philosophy that I was indoctrinated with. I guess during World War II, after getting out of the Air Corps, philosophically I began to try to deal with things. My problem came when I read the Sermon on the Mount. I had been familiar with it all my life, and it did not mesh with war. The question became how could a Christian justify war and aggression. I wrestled with that a long time. Finally I met some Quakers. I didn't know much about Quakers, I found out that they were pacifists. I met some who believed in finding other ways to solve problems. They had a great impact on me.

I decided I wanted to become a Quaker until I found out you just couldn't walk up and become a Quaker, you had to go through a lot of talk. I decided not to go through that. At that point, I began to really develop my own philosophy. I guess it's not my own, but a meshing of the others. And it seems to me that what I came down on is that we somehow need to move into an era, and a feeling, where there is understanding. We should put more effort into finding solutions, understanding and being just. I've looked at situations, done some traveling, in the Middle East and Africa, Europe. I look at the situation in the Middle East. For five thousand years there has been no peace. I don't accept that. Here in America we have every race, religion, culture. What a great opportunity for us to demonstrate that people can live together in fairness, in justice. We must demonstrate that in this country so the world can look at us as an example.

To be very honest, having worked all my life, stopping and doing nothing would be such a shock and change that it would be upsetting to me. To say nothing of the fact that I'd probably drive my wife crazy if I were around under foot all the time. I haven't given any thought to stopping working because I'm continually finding new projects to pursue.

Portraits of Passion: Aging, Defying the Myth

The one thing that has worked for me. I make a full commitment. In my consulting, this is why I very carefully choose my clients. You have to put in proposals to this and that, and as I put it in the proposal, I'm evaluating the person, the institution that I work with. Once I've made a commitment, I'm committed to have them successful, because their success is my success. This is why you have to limit. You can't do everything. But quality, support at whatever you're doing has been the one thing that has driven me. I took jobs that no one wanted. When I went to work at the State Department of Education, I was a consultant. It was a professional job. But I made a commitment to do it well. Maybe it's old fashioned, but it's the way that's worked for me.

I would say that getting old, I feel that maybe health is an issue and one should look after their health. I've tried not to go to extremes. I also think I've been fortunate to be in reasonably good health. I can say that I've been fortunate as long as I'm able to make the contribution I want to make.

I believe that we should have goals and we should work at them every day. And never forget that as an individual we should be out there ready to help support the kinds of things that are going to make this country the kind of place that we want it to be.

PART FIVE

Body, Mind, and Spirit

Enola Dundy Maxwell

CHAPTER TWENTY-SIX

Enola Dundy Maxwell

Enola Maxwell was born on August 30, 1919 in Baton Rouge, Louisiana. She has three children, 13 grandchildren, and three great-grandchildren. Enola has been the executive director of the Potrero Hill Neighborhood House since 1972. In 1967, she was commissioned as the first Lay Minister by the San Francisco Presbetery. She was Peace delegate to Vancouver, Canada in 1970 and to the USSR in 1973, appointed to the San Francisco Human Rights Commission in 1976, and was invited to tour the People's Republic of China with the U.S. China Peoples Friendship Association in 1977. Enola received a commendation from the Speaker of the California Assembly for her work at the Potrero Hill Health Clinic.

Enola has won innumerable awards, and belongs to several activist groups representing women and many disenfranchised groups. Some of her other honors include: Women's Leadership Award from Alliance Against Women's Oppression; Honorary Nominee: Women on the Move - Anti-Defamation League; Mary McLeod Bethune Centennial Award from the National Council of Negro Women; Martin Luther King Jr. Humanitarian Award; National Women's Political Caucus Award; Omega Boys' Club Award for Distinguished and Dedicated Service; honored by Congresswoman Nancy Pelosi in the United States Congressional Record: 1987.

———— ❖ ————

Portraits of Passion: Aging, Defying the Myth

Well, what I've done, if I've done anything, is to have a commitment to justice and equality. I intend to work for that as long as I live. Helping people in need and trying to pass the word and asking for justice for all people.

What is justice? Where is justice? Where is equality? Those are my issues, not so much for people, but for America, for what America stands for. Yeah, let's make the Constitution, our proclamations, a reality. There's a wide discrepancy, a very wide discrepancy. And wherever I can I point out these discrepancies to whoever will listen, I try to make a difference.

I was born in Baton Rouge, Louisiana. My grandmother and grandfather, they stood up for justice. They stood up whenever necessary, and told the man how they felt about it.

I grew up as a Baptist. My parents and grandparents belonged to the NAACP. All of my life I've been a member of the church and the NAACP. So I grew up with that kind of orientation and my parents were into that orientation.

My grandmother was 40 years old before she learned to write her name. But there was not anybody I've ever known with so much pride. You don't need to be educated to have pride. You don't need to be rich to have pride. And so they taught us this, pride and holding your head up. I patterned myself after my grandparents more or less. My father and my mother was kind of a silent type, always there, and very strong.

The Scriptures meant a lot to me. And I think this is why I feel about some things the way I do. We learned to read when I was growing up, before we went to school. Because you had to recite your Bible verse every Sunday morning. Of course, my attitude toward Christianity changed over the years. It became a little different because I have ceased to believe some of the things that I was taught. But I still believe in the teachings of Jesus Christ.

Sometimes people tell me that I made a difference in their lives, some of the kids that you work with over the years. You've seen them go to college and become educated. We have among them good fathers and good mothers, housewives, bus drivers, photographers, and various and sundry people that sometimes you don't even know about. You get a letter from France and somebody says, they learned photography, they started in our photography class. Now they're taking pictures in France. It gives you a feeling that somebody was helped. It paid off for some, and maybe, who knows who all it paid off.

I was not a healthy person in my youth. I was unhealthy and I just really had no idea that I would ever live to be 40, let alone 70. The older I got the more healthy I became. If you're not healthy you can't do very much. I missed a lot of time when other kids were in school. I had so many problems, but the spirit of Jesus Christ gave me the courage to keep doing whatever I could and I began to pray this prayer, "Lord, help me to do what I can do for myself." It helps me overcome a lot of things. That's another thing about misfortunes. How you turn a negative into a positive. You go on and you don't allow these negative things to affect you for any length of time. You're thinking about another way to deal with this situation. So you don't have time to dwell on it.

You treat others with respect and how they treat you is their problem. That's how I learned to overcome a lot of racist attitude and a lot of racism. When I came to this house, every week there was a meeting here about all the horrible things that I was doing here. They were going to sue the city if they didn't take away this house. The police said, we're going to be watching you. Well, I thought that was a great idea. If you're watching you can see what I am doing, but you can also see what I'm not doing, so the police became friendly. We weren't doing anything. The firemen were here all the time.

When I put in my application to work at the Potrero House, they said, "You don't have a Masters, or a social worker degree." The Presbyterian Church was social minded at that time. It was in 1968. The Potrero House belongs to the Presbyterian Church, so when this job became vacant, I applied for the job. Without the support of the people, I mean, everybody was there to support me. With patience and perseverance, you don't know any defeat.

Back in Louisiana about 50 years ago, it got to the point where I had to make a decision whether I was going on to be a Christian or whether I was going on to live in poverty. I couldn't be a Christian and live in poverty. I had been a Christian all my life. Now, it was hard to give up being a Christian, so I had to give up poverty. I never had any money but I wasn't poor. I had three children. I couldn't bring them up in poverty, so our needs had to be met.

Poverty is a handicap, a serious handicap. All kinds of things happen to you in poverty. I was still poor, but my children didn't know we were poor. I didn't want them to know. I did not want to bring up my children on the basis that we could do or not do things because of money. The difference is in what you need and what you want. All our needs had to be supplied. I made this pact with the Lord.

As you get older, you're really more free. If you have the strength to work, then I think you should work. If you can't work in a job that pays money, there are so many people out there that you can use your skill, your patience, and your kindness. It gives you a feeling of worth and a feeling of having something to do. And you should continue your education. There's so many new things to learn. You can't learn it all, but you can learn some new things and new ideas.

Nobody calls me old. I never think about myself as being old, and I don't think anybody else does. We have seniors in our program, some of them are younger than I am, and you have to try to tell them that just because you're old there's no point in being so demanding. Every car doesn't have to stop for you to cross the street. You have to try to live in such in a way that the young people will feel that you care about them. It's a two-way street.

If seniors become demanding, and are egged on by people with jobs, and people who are going to school, who want to teach old people how to be old, it's ridiculous situation. If you're not there being old and demanding and in need, those people will be out of work. So you pretend all of this so they can keep their jobs. But please don't succumb to this kind of thing. The locksmith, everybody, the police department, they have classes. They come over here and teach how to protect yourself. If we listened to them, you'd be afraid to go out of the house, you'd be afraid to stay in the house, afraid to take a purse with you. What in the heck are you going to do without a purse? It's just so crazy, in my opinion. Instructing seniors how to live and take care of themselves is a whole growth industry. We're big business now.

I've been an invalid about four times in my life. It came to me that when I was making all these determinations about eliminating the word "can't", and accepting things, examining the reality, I had to ask myself what is it about this situation that I could change? Do I have to accept it or do I have to change it? I start searching for a way of life, Christianity as a way of life. There were several things I had to have, quietness of the spirit, freedom of the soul, to be free. And whatever disturbs the quietness of my spirit, requires re-examination.

My present goal is to help this child care center, and start a summer school here and gradually turn it into a permanent everyday school. Because education to me is the key. You need a basic education, something on which to build the training on. So many of our people are unemployed, and they're unemployable. We have tutorial programs here, after- school programs everyday. We have the Omega Boys Club, a college-oriented club. We want to give these kids the basics and the motivation that education is the key, maybe not to a better job, not to higher pay, but it's the key to life and living and freedom of the soul and freedom of the spirit.

James F. T. Bugental

CHAPTER TWENTY-SEVEN

James F. T. Bugental

James Bugental is a writer, lecturer, group leader, and humanistic psychologist. He conducts classes and workshops in the U.S. and Europe. He received his B.S. degree from West Texas State College in 1940, his M.A. from George Peabody College in 1941, and his Ph.D. at Ohio State University in 1948.

He is the recipient of the first Rollo May Award of the Mentor Society for "contributions to the literary pursuit". He is an emeritus adjunct faculty member at the Saybrook Institute in San Francisco, and an emeritus clinical lecturer at the Department of Psychiatry at Stanford University Medical School. From 1989 to 1990, he was Visiting Distinguished Professor at the California School of Professional Psychology at Berkeley, California. He has taught and lectured to dozens of university and professional groups and has been a keynote speaker at over a score of major seminars.

Dr. Bugental's extensive list of published works include The Art of the Psychotherapist, *chosen as a main selection of the Psychotherapy Book Review,* The Search for Authenticity: An Existential-Analytic Approach to Psychotherapy, *and* The Human Possibility.

He has received many awards and certificates for his contribution to the discipline of clinical psychology. He is married and has three children.

❖

Portraits of Passion: Aging, Defying the Myth

You never get to the end of it. The road keeps opening up over the next horizon. So I'm at work on a new book that will in some ways go way beyond what I've written before, some ways refute some of what I've written before, and some ways extend it. Ideas just happen to me. They just keep erupting, emerging, no more than does a wood search for new trees. It evolves.

Rollo May talks about the epoch into which we're born. My father reached his years of maturity during the Great Depression. It knocked him down again and again. That was very hard for him to take because he was a proud man. He wanted to be the breadwinner. He wanted to do it all. Again and again, his big plans, his efforts were knocked down. And yet he always bounced back with new optimism, new energy. My mother was the same in many ways. During the same period, she wanted to be a concert pianist and had the talent for it, but opted for a different career. She was disappointed, angered about things, but would bounce back again with new optimism. I think that was terribly important. My earliest learning about disappointment was from the way they met the challenges of their lives. I learned it was not the end of the line.

In my last year in high school, I was always one of the nerds, one of the outsiders. The journalism professor made me the editor of the annual, which was a powerful change in my image of myself. Suddenly, I couldn't say, I couldn't do it, I'm on the outside. I did it. I did it very well, and it had lasting effect on me. In my life there were a succession of mentors. I can think of a scoutmaster, a professor when I was finishing my undergraduate work, several professors in graduate school. Professionally there quite a few namely, George Kelly, Abraham Maslow, Carl Rogers, Rollo May.

I retired from active practice in 1987. I am now focused on teaching and writing. The personal payoff for me for my continuous work is that I get fresh perspectives on things. I certainly like to see a client who has made a major turnaround, viewing his or her life in a fresh way. That's part of why I'm still going on, because there are so many gratifications.

I'm leaving the middle of next month for a tour, stopping in Denver, Pennsylvania, Connecticut, New York and Cape Cod, to do programs. That's very, very gratifying, and harks back to that early thing, being an outsider, a nerd, sort of an odd duck.

Now I'm an insider, I'm valued. I'm not an oddball, which gives me the courage then to do oddball things. Isn't that interesting? Because I feel secure that I'm valued, then I can do things that are fresh, that are provocative.

I like being old. There are so damn many things that used to seem heavy and tremendously weighing on me that I don't care about now. I don't see why I wasted so much energy on it. It's all a learning experience. Carl Rogers in his last years did something that I always wished he hadn't, and that is to say that he was still "young". I think in that way he missed the fact that he was old, that he was well-matured. He had it made. I don't know if Carl ever realized what a tremendous change he made in his latter years. In the 80's he was talking almost 180 degrees from his earlier position. I can't think he was young. He was old and full of freshness.

Some people fight aging. They feel that only being young has meaning. They feel, "somehow I've got to hang onto being young." Aging is a natural process, if you fight a natural process, then you're not going to do it very well.

My divorce was a very painful thing. It has affected me in many ways. The first thing was in changing my image of myself, that I would be divorced, that I would break up with this woman with whom I'd shared so much. I had to see myself and the whole process of commitment and relationship in new ways. I was around fifty, and at that time I was seeing myself as old. I made this change being old, and after the divorce, there was a sense of liberation, of freedom. Not because my first wife was mean or domineering, but just because I was making new relationships. Now when I look at someone who is 50, 52 years old, they're kids.

I value greatly the human experience. That experience is very broadly interpreted. I have room in that for something we can call spirit or spiritual. It doesn't fit into any established religion. I had periods when I was very involved in organized religion. It was about the time I was finishing graduate school, so I was about 32. My philosophical base is constantly evolving. It's not a fixed thing. It's more a humane concern for the whole of human beings as an entity, a sense that we are at a very early stage, very primitive stage in understanding our own nature. And what is possible is that it's never-ending, it's opening, it's infinite.

I'll be seventy-five this year. A lot of the things that seemed so important, getting approval, doing everything by the book, or not by the book in other cases, a lot of the things that use up emotional energy when you were young just aren't worth the trouble. So it's a freer now. My work is very much a source of nourishment, of renewal, for keeping me fresh. If you're lucky you'll find work that is continually renewing. If you're in a dead-end job, get the hell out and find something that does it for you.

Another thing that helps the aging process is having something that turns your perspective beyond the moment. I have a lot of aches and pains in my joints, and if I were only living in this moment, it would be pretty debilitating. They're a nuisance, but they're not crucial, in some sense they're irrelevant.

My passion now is the exploration of the infinite possibility in the human experience. The satisfaction of trying to rescue our image of ourselves, pulling something out that I can put into some kind of shape. Not just in my writing, or in my professional life, the exploration goes on between my wife and me, and with my daughter. It's all interwoven. I feel I have optimism, this upbeat thing that my parents manifested so clearly that I feel I've carried on. My central theme is discovery. Optimism says there's always more to discover.

The most important thing in helping me maintain this optimism, in confronting and accepting that I'm aging, that I'm approaching death, is my relationship with my wife. It's been support, in the sense of comfort. It's support in the sense of confrontation, a sharedness. Recently I had what we thought at first was a minor stroke. It turns out happily that it was not. But we found we really had to face it.

The funny part was that I would've said I dealt with all of the issues, but it's very different when it's in the moment right now. My wife, just her steady presence, her openness, was tremendously important to me dealing with those issues. She can't reassure me it won't happen, but she can reassure me of her standing by, not leaving, not leaving emotionally.

Jerry Jampolsky

CHAPTER TWENTY-EIGHT

Jerry Jampolsky

Psychiatrist, Gerald G. Jampolsky, M.D., has gained international recognition for his work with children who have catastrophic illness. In 1975, he established the Center for Attitudinal Healing in Tiburon, California. Jerry describes his work at the Center as "spiritual psychotherapy," where health is defined as inner peace and healing as letting go of fear. He sees this work as a supplement to, rather than a replacement for, traditional medical treatment.

Dr. Jampolsky is a graduate of Stanford Medical School, a former faculty member of the University of California School of Medicine in San Francisco, and has held fellowships in child psychiatry at Langley Porter Neuropsychiatric Institute.

Jerry has published numerous books including the best selling, Love is Letting Go Of Fear. Love is the Answer, *co-authored by Jerry and Diane V. Ciricnione, was published in March 1990. His newest book published by Bantam came out in November 1990 titled,* One Person Can Make a Difference. *In connection with his work at the Center, Jerry has appeared on many major television programs including* 60 Minutes, The Today Show, *and* The Phil Donahue Show.

Jerry Jampolsky founded the project, "Children As Teachers of Peace", in 1982. He feels that the simplicity, clear vision, and hope of children on the issues of peace will serve as a reminder of the essence of peace that is in all of us.

---❖---

Portraits of Passion: Aging, Defying the Myth

I believe that life has to do with vitality in the present moment. I think we're here not to relive the past or be uncertain or fear the future, but we're here to live with the utmost vitality and zest in the most giving way we can. It means letting go of the shadows of yesterday and recognize that age has nothing to do with our chronology, but it has to do with our heart and how full our heart is. Some of the most vital people I know have been people in their 70's and 80's who have a similar way of looking at life, as if this is the only day in the world and you were born to this day and everything you see is brand new. They're just in awe and speaking from an inspiration, because most of these people I know have also a connection with a higher power. They feel really inspired that they're here to help and love other people.

The problem that most people have as they get older is they get concerned about their limitations. They get focused on bodily ailments, they get focused on their fear of dying, they get focused on the fact that many people are dying, and there are not so many people left that were our friends. To me, they're concentrating on the wrong things. When you concentrate on how blessed we are each day and can look back only on the positive things, you have what a dear friend of mine, Bill Thetford, called celestial amnesia. Then I think we can come with full vitality and we're still here for the same reasons: to help, to be kind, to assist other people, to love and to know that everyone comes into our life as a teacher of forgiveness. I think we're here to be the light of the world, to express that creation's love and light.

My parents' goal in this world was to have three sons and to have them have the advantages that they didn't have. They both migrated from the old country, and they had very strong work ethics. They ran a little shop. They got up at 7 in the morning, they were there until 10 o'clock at night. I think they really cared about other people. They had problems in receiving, but they're the kind of people who would really make sure that the iceman got a present at Christmas time. I think my parents felt a lot of guilt and it weighed on them. They had a philosophy different from my philosophy, but I bought into it for many years because I was a dutiful son -- that yesterday was awful, today's horrendous and tomorrow's going to be worse. It's very hard to enjoy the moment, when life is here to suffer for the future. Maybe they were good teachers for me to say, hey, that's not what I want from my life. I don't need to suffer anymore. You have happiness and joy when you realize that happiness is your natural state.

I really didn't have any mentors growing up like most people have. One person who I remember as sort of a father figure was when I was an intern. As a kid and as an adult I was sort of a clumsy clod. I was a dyslexic, if I was cutting turkey it would end up going on the floor, that kind of stuff. I was interning in surgery, and this guy really liked me and had faith in me. I was the best intern for that year and he wanted me to become a surgeon. He saw the best in me and didn't see my faults. Certainly today, people that I really respect are Mother Theresa and the Dalai Lama. Those are two people who have had a tremendous influence on my life in terms of their day-to-day demonstration of living, their spiritual principles, and certainly Albert Schweitzer.

I have a new book coming out. It's called *How One Person Can Make a Difference*. There are stories of some famous people, and not so famous, how they're making a difference. We need models. I think it's helpful to have as many as you can. When you see people doing these things, the world doesn't have to know about it. It all comes down not to what we've done in this world, but how much love we've given. People who have found that peace do not have to tell you about it. You can tell by their presence.

I was with someone yesterday who was there when we started the Center for Attitudinal Healing. She volunteered for me for many years. She developed cancer about six years ago. I hadn't seen her for awhile. I can be with her and give her some of my sustenance and share my love with her. When two people are getting together as friends, as we are helping each other, this is the highest form of joy a human being can experience.

I was an atheist and very attached to guilt and making judgments when I came across a book called, *The Course of Miracles*. It became a spiritual transformation for me. That was a world-shattering event in that it changed my life completely: to live a life getting a piece of God as the only goal, to see everyone who comes into my life as a teacher of forgiveness. Forgiveness is my function. Listen to my heart, tell me what to think, say, and do, because I was always making judgments on my experiences. So that really had a tremendous effect on me.

Life is totally different for me. I was totally involved in a life that was, trying to get as much as I can. It was a material world, how much money I had in the bank, what kind of car I drove, where I was in my community in terms of comparison with other people. I was involved

Portraits of Passion: Aging, Defying the Myth

in a world of competition and running very hard, things my parents taught me. I have a new kind of life where I really have a feeling of trust and faith, of a higher power, that God will never leave me comfortless. So I'm still struggling each day not to be attached to anything that I have. There are days that I am attached, but I know I'm heading in the right direction.

The world's been too hooked into productiveness: how many books you've written, how many companies you're on the board of directors of. I think that we ought to be hooked into the content of our lives. There has been more concentration on the physical/ material world than on the real essence of our self, our spiritual self. I think that's a whole different kind of motivation.

The question why some people age well and others do not has I think, much to do with fear. One of the saddest things to do is to go to a retirement home and see elderly people who have been dumped there, who are isolated from society, feeling useless and deprived and are concentrating on death. I think one of the biggest fears that people have in the aging process is dying. I think when we let go of that one, overcome that, and realize that life really is eternal, then our whole life becomes different. So I think our fear of death causes a lot of problems.

The most important thing I could tell another person about aging is forget all the things that you thought you learned about aging, all the things you got from your culture, from parents and school, all the things you got from your observations. Forget all the things you think you know about aging as having a negative connotation. Imagine if you will that you have no memory of what aging is all about, total amnesia for that. The number on it really makes no difference. You still have to have a purpose in being here. When you know that your purpose is to love, forgive, and be helpful to others you will always be young in heart and in that sense, ageless.

Bella Lewitzky

CHAPTER TWENTY-NINE

Bella Lewitzky

Bella Lewitzky is the West Coast's leading representative of modern dance, and has been changing the landscape of her chosen art for more than five decades. Her career was launched with the famed Lester Horton. She became Horton's colleague and founded with him the Dance Theater of Los Angeles in 1946. In 1966, she formed the Lewitzky Dance Company, with whom she performed well into her sixties and for whom she continues to expend her considerable talent and energy. Under her artistic guidance the Company has become one of the leading international modern dance companies performing to critical acclaim around the world.

Since 1982, Bella has been immersed in the creation of The Dance Gallery, her lifelong dream for a state-of-the-art facility to nurture the dance performer, choreographer, and audience. The realization of this dream will place Bella Lewitzky, Los Angeles, and the West Coast at the cutting edge of the dance world.

Although she no longer performs, her creative energy continues unabated. She has not stopped caring about her art form, a fact born out by the numerous awards she has received for service to the dance, and the advisory and honorary positions she holds on boards and councils of prestigious art institutions across the nation.

------- ❖ -------

I don't think of what I do as working. What I do is living. So the question should be, why do you keep on living? Because that is what I'm born to do, to keep on living. My life and my work are inseparable.

Portraits of Passion: Aging, Defying the Myth

They always have been.

The value system in which I grew up fostered the things I have mentioned. I thought every single person had exactly the same support system and permission to move forward with their life in a creative way. It never entered my mind that I grew up in a singular or atypical way. I never thought of it as being uncommon, for which I'll be eternally grateful. I lived in a family of people that were poor in the material sense, and very wealthy in everything else that had to do with what makes up one's life.

My family was actually almost a cellular family, in that all of the people who would have made up our extended family were in Russia, or on another coast. I personally had never met them. My father was a philosopher, a humanist, a Sunday painter. My mother was also empathetic to those things, so that art was in our home as bread was on our table. We were extremely poor, but we never suffered from the feeling of being a "poor family," because of the amount of emotional support we got. There was an incredible freedom as I grew up. We had literature in our home, we had music in our home. We had my father's painting in our home, and when I decided that I wanted to be a dancer no one in my family turned to me and said, "But what will you do to earn a living?" They simply said, "Wonderful Bella! Go forth, do what you can do, just do it well and know what it is that you want."

My father was a socialist, so was my mother. It was not a matter of political belief, as much as humanitarian belief, meaning that the things that mattered to them were to somehow be able to make all of society, not just themselves or their brothers or their immediate family or even their children, but to make all of the world free from hunger, want, disease and war. They had total charity in their hearts.

I can remember my father during the days of what was called The Great Depression. I refused to be anything but angry with the idea of the Depression being described as great, because great has more than one meaning. It was large, it wasn't great. It was pitifully horrible. I remember my father going to families in our neighborhood who were unemployed, as was the major part of the world in those days, and turning the gas on and turning the electricity on, turning the water on so that these people could survive. He lived his life as a humanitarian.

My immediate family has had the greatest influenced on me. Outside of that, it would be teachers I had met. I've never really tried to examine this, I think I was influenced by maybe three or four teachers, and their passion for their subjects. Through them my world widened to something I would never have known before. Although, I didn't recognize it at the time. I was just in awe of how much that person had given me, and so that kind of gift-giving was probably very important in shaping the way I grew up.

The best kind of reward that one could have is being able to serve an art form with its demands, its disappointments, and its successes. There is something far greater than the individual involved in this. You start out to do something and you say it's your work, and then when you get through and you look at it on a stage and you say, "I wonder where that came from?" It's almost as though I have divested myself of what it was that I did. It is no longer my personal possession. That's a very strange and interesting phenomena that I think most artists experience. The teaching part of it, I love equally well I would say. Although if I had to choose one over the other I think the act of creativity cannot be topped.

Creation is exactly what the word says it is: making something that wasn't there until you made it. That is a major act in anyone's life, I think. But teaching did something for me very interesting. I tend to be a humanist, not because my family said that was what I should be, because I dipped into all kinds of things. I rejected what I would have called the supernatural. So I dealt with things in a different way. That's one of the things that being poor does teach you, a certain level of realism.

But I did find that there is a form of reincarnation. All the gifts poured into me and the things which I have added to them, I can pass on. Life continues for me in a very interesting way. I can look at it and say, there is a continuum and there is continuity, as long as there are those among of us who are in a position to help create it. And I do feel an indebtedness. I wouldn't say it's a burden, but rather a joy.

I remember as a teenager, being convinced that death would never happen, and that I could certainly correct all the ills in the world. One gets through that phase only by bumps. My mother was ill and that was very difficult for our family. The not so Great Depression was another very severe crisis that shook up our family. I was also personally effected when I was involved in debating the immorality of the House Un-American Activities Committee during the 50's. I have always been amused that somehow, someone could think that by dancing I could overthrow the world. I never even thought of it in terms of morality,

Portraits of Passion: Aging, Defying the Myth

I just thought of it as being a wonderful attribute. But it was a bruising experience to find out how easily one can be victimized, and how helpless one can become. That was a hard lesson, and one which shaped much of what I did following that period. But it never deflected me from my path, because I think art is all-encompassing. Maybe I shouldn't speak for all art, but I assume it's true of all art. My art certainly can encompass the bumps.

I cannot abide categories. I do not like little boxes. So I tend to step aside from things which are organized in that fashion. I have never been comfortable with it, yet I would not say I live an unguided life. I am directed by the things life has taught me and that I was hopefully intelligent enough to absorb. I've always hoped that I've been able to learn from my mistakes.

I would say I draw from my own experience and the experiences of others. I have never been interested in an organized religion. Although I would say, probably I would be defined as a humanist. I do believe that people are responsible for people. I do believe that we can make a difference even though it's very difficult at times to do that, but I think people move people.

I think what happens in the dance world is that if you grow to be my age, you suddenly become venerable. You're excused for a lot of things. I have been able to function fairly well, although I think I'm falling apart incrementally, piece by piece. But as long as I know what it is, I can deal with it. But when I began to be asked, "Would I speak on aging?" I went, "What? Why?" I never saw myself in that context. It was alarming, on the one hand, and on the other it gave me a heck of a lot of insight. Because I think what I realized is those of us who have reached the age that I have reached think of ourselves in a very different age bracket than we are, if we think of age at all.

I tend not to think of age. It's just never interested me, even when I was very young. I don't know that I actually put a numerical value on age. I never thought, I am old, with the negative implications that are placed on being old. I didn't think of that. But later I thought there are probably two things that are truths and equally true: there are those of us who see ourselves as we function, which is not as old people, and there are those who look and see us as old people. That was kind of an interesting stepping stone for me, when I realized that the world must see me as an old person. I am in their terms, old.

I don't spend much time looking back. I think the kind of work which I do has a way of keeping my body as well as my mind resilient, because I move physically in what I do. I would say that if you think of yourself as retired, there is an age about 50 or 60 when one says, "This is it, you have now passed youth, you are now at the point where you are retired." If you then put yourself into a rocking chair, your physical body will conform to that, your bones will take over the shape of that rocking chair. They will stop being what they need to be, which is to have the capacity to move well, and I'm not talking about aerobics, just a person who moves.

If there's one thing I think a dancer knows it has to be that the body, the emotions, and the mind are one unit. If you are sick, you're an extraordinary person if you also feel good. On the other hand, if you're well, you're bound to feel better. If you accept retirement as meaning that you stop doing anything, you are then just sitting and waiting to die, which is a terrible waste of time. I had an interesting experience with a group of people on the first cultural exchange to China. I was treated with singular regard. I thought, what on earth is happening? I'm usually treated like everybody else. It finally dawned on me that China has a history of worship of their ancestors, older people. I was the oldest member of our group. So I immediately thought, well, it's not something singular about me, it's my age. It was a very funny experience.

Life for me has remained an ongoing process. As long as each day remains productive and creative, I will probably continue until I cannot continue. I think people age well who simply have not stopped living. They still have curiosity, they intake information, and if they're very fortunate, they can give information.

This is not an aging process. It's a process of taking everything that has come to you in life, doubling its value, and being able to partake of it. There are some gifts in growing to be old that come just by the number of years you've lived, that mean you have accrued certain kinds of wisdom just through experience that younger people haven't had. You can watch that when you see young people staggered by an incident that has set them off their track. You go, "Hey, there's tomorrow, and after tomorrow, there's the day after tomorrow." Also, if you are disease ridden, it is very difficult to age well. Because your entire mental/emotional set is bent upon simply trying to endure. And that is hard. It would take enormous creativity to surmount that. But there have been people who have done just that.

Portraits of Passion: Aging, Defying the Myth

My work is the major part of what keeps me perking along. If I've done a good dance, it's a rejoiceful time for me. It's really celebratory. When I teach well, I come in and I can say, "You taught a damn good class, you passed on a lot of information." I'm a disciplined person, but it's commitment more than discipline. I'm a very committed person to myself, to my ideals, to my art form, to politics, to the things I believe in, to my family. I am totally committed to my belief system. I am committed to my ethical system.

I have no problem with aging. I feel that once you have passed a certain age, everyday is a reward. You can wake up and say, "By God, I'm 74 and ten days!", it is absolutely bonus points. It's wonderful to have the opportunity to get beyond a certain point.

Richard Eskite, Photographer

Moira Jackson

CHAPTER THIRTY

Moira Jackson

Moira Jackson was born eighty years ago in Albany, New York. She received her education at Holy Names Academy in Seattle, Washington; University of Washington, University of Minnesota, and City College of San Francisco. She is a widow and has three children.

Moira has held many positions of importance in her career: industrial editor, Executive Secretary of the American-Italy Society, Executive Director for Young Audiences of San Francisco, Commissioner of the San Francisco Commission on Aging, Senior Senator - California Senior Legislature, California Commissioner on Aging, and Chairman formerly of the White House Conference Committee of San Francisco. She served as Congresswoman Nancy Pelosi's Senior Intern in Washington D.C., and as a member of the Mayor's Committee for Affordable Housing. She continues to be an active advocate for senior rights and care.

———— ❖ ————

I want a purpose in life. My background, everything I have done has tended towards this end. I find that it is a very satisfying sort of thing that I am doing. I love to travel. I have an itchy foot. I could never be content to simply play bridge, lead a recreational sort of life without purpose.

For a good part of my life I don't think I was contributing, now I can choose what I'll do. I now have some freedom to be able to make decisions about what I want to do with my life.

My mother was very supportive. My father, because of the kind of person he was and the kind of background he had, was not as supportive as he might have been. I'm sure he wanted to be. I came from a generation where girls were very much expected to follow a certain pattern, especially if they were in the middle class. We were suppose to marry, to have children. Careers were a very remote possibility. I was suppose to make the most of my education and my opportunities but I wasn't suppose to do very much with it. The early seeds of being productive were planted by my mother. I would say also that I had teachers who fostered it. One of my early mentors was Sister Mary Patrick at Holy Names Academy in Seattle. I had her in some of my high school classes in Latin. She was very much a friend, in fact she was a friend throughout my life as long as she lived.

Because Seattle was a very conservative city and it still is to some extent, I proceeded to get married when I was just barely 21. We later had 3 children. The marriage did not work out. We got a divorce and I spent the next several years just fighting to maintain myself and my youngest child because I really wasn't trained for anything. When I met my second husband, he was a brilliant man. He was also a writer. We were very much in love and eventually we married. My whole life changed. Not a great deal financially because neither one of us were money makers. But I had the support which I had never had in my life before. I learned a great from him.

Because my husband was much older than I, and because I took care of him in his last illness at home, I realized as he grew old and frail how many services were needed. I knew had he not had me to see to it that he had the things that he needed he really would have been in a very bad situation. I felt when he died that I wanted to help the elderly, not just because I was getting there myself, but also because I had seen what it had meant to my husband. I had never done anything in public. I had never been one for volunteer work. It was quite an eye opener for me. So, at 65 I started to get more into a social-service type job, and became more of an activist. I made up my mind as a kind of memorial to my husband and as something I wished to do, that this was the way I wanted to go. My whole life reversed itself. I had been quite conservative. I had been a registered Republican for all of my life. Not for any good reason except I just did it. Since then I have changed parties. I have become much more liberal in my outlook, much more outspoken.

I have been a Roman Catholic all of my life. I am fortunate in belonging to a parish. I was away from the church for a number of years and then returned to it, although my husband had been a Baptist and an Agnostic for most of his life. I had wished that he would have a little more faith, but he eventually became a Catholic too, and joined me in the last few years of his life. I have great support at St. Teresa's because we have a splendid pastor. His name is Father Peter Sammon. As a Christian, Christ says to us "As I have done, so you must do." They are strong words and it is not an easy path sometimes. But it is the one that, as Christians, we feel obliged to follow.

When my husband died I also thought somewhat of going into a contemplative order, if they would accept me at that age, and doing that which would have meant isolating myself from, to some extent, from family and friends. It was about that time that Sister Kathleen said to me, "Moira, you have a great gift with people." And I though "Dear Lord, you must be telling me something." If I have a gift with people, than I better not be immuring myself in a convent.

Today there are quite a number of payoffs for the work that I do. In the first place, it has given me a position in the city which I should not otherwise have had; which is very gratifying and which I hadn't especially expected. I am in a time where I am losing so many of my friends, one of the detrimental things that happens as we get to my age is that we lose a lot of the friends who have been our support throughout the years.

I think a great many things are clearer to me now. I think we are much less inclined to judge others harshly or ourselves. I think it is wonderful to be able to have this retrospective glance at all of our ages, and what we have been in various ages, because to me it's as if I have lived several lives. It's as if I became a different person at different ages.

I think health is a very important factor because it affects us not only physically, but mentally at all ages. I know my Mother was a very sensible women as far as nutrition was concerned. I think we learn from that and I have always tried to be reasonably sensible. Some people don't have quite the genes of others. Some people haven't had the nutrition that they needed in their earlier lives which does make a great deal of difference, or perhaps at other times in their lives they may not have had the support they needed and they may not have kept themselves as well as they could. It is very important to me, because I live alone and I want to remain independent if I possibly can. I try to take as good care of myself as I can. That's why I try to get to an

Portraits of Passion: Aging, Defying the Myth

aerobics class, three times a week.

My work is part of keeping active and keeping fit, because it keeps me going mentally. I tend to be a little bit absent minded and forgetful. Sometimes I'm forced to take stock of myself and just say "now this won't do, come on let's try to improve it."

I review periodically. For instance, this coming year I don't intend to take on quite as much as I have, because I have to pay attention to certain things here at home. I have served a number of times in the California Senior Legislature as a member of the Joint Rules Committee. I'm not going to do that. I have served a number of times on the Legislative Committee which is really the thing that I enjoy doing in Sacramento because it means working for various pieces of legislation that affect the elderly. I'm not going to be doing that because I feel I must keep enough time here for myself.

I had a burn-out period this year. Depression is not my thing, generally I'm pretty optimistic. But I had a period that I was depressed and I just thought "Okay, roll with it, you've been with it before." So I didn't do a lot of the things that I should have done. I thought "I can't help it." I have a safe-guard mechanism so that when things go awry I don't go awry but I kind of roll with it.

In October, I'll be 80. I'm looking forward to that birthday. Father Sammon is going to say a Mass in the afternoon, on a Saturday, and my family is all coming down from Seattle. It may be that my stepson and his wife will come over from Texas and a lot of my friends here in the city will be there. I'm looking forward to that. As far as long-term goals for myself, I am realistic and at 80 I don't know if I'm going to live to be 90. I certainly don't want to live to be 100. One never knows these days. I often say "Dear Lord, when you want me, please take me fast." Which is what most elderly people say.

There are certain things we do that we wished we hadn't: refined, changed, obliterated entirely. But on the other hand, had I done those I might not have met the man whom I eventually married, which would have been a great loss to me. So I feel, "che sara sara."

Jorgen Bernard Jensen

CHAPTER THIRTY-ONE

Jorgen Bernard Jensen

Born in Stockton, California, on March 25, 1908, Jorgen B. Jensen is known as a teacher, lecturer, chiropractor, clinical nutritionist, and iridiagnostician. He received his D.C. from the West Coast Chiropractic College in 1929. He received his Doctor of Naturopathy from the American School of Naturopathy in New York in 1931. In 1932, he received his diploma in the Science of Iridiagnosis, a technique in which he has been on the forefront. He subsequently received his Ph.D. in Clinical Nutrition from the School of Humanistic Studies in San Diego, California, in 1984.

He has traveled the world over, and has lectured in over 50 countries. He has been in private practice since 1929, and has written numerous articles and books related to nutrition and health. He was director of an 85-bed sanitarium at Hidden Valley Health Ranch in Escondido, California. During the last half century he has lectured to over 300,000 patients and students throughout the world. He has made numerous television appearances and produces videos and movies about health.

Dr. Jensen holds many certificates of scholastic recognition from schools and institutes, and holds honorary degrees throughout the United States and around the world. In 1982, he was presented the Dag Hammarskjold Award by Pax Mundi.

———— ❖ ————

Portraits of Passion: Aging, Defying the Myth

I think that the idea of growing old is a misnomer. If you are growing you're expanding, developing, working, and productive. That's growing. But when they say you're growing old, you see, that's another thought. So that really, they don't go together. Now you can grow old, and I think some people grow old too young. Because there's times now that I try to reconcile with my age, trying to make readjustments that would fit my body and what I'm capable of doing and so forth. Mentally, I'm still capable of jumping a six-foot fence. However, realistically I feel that I should adjust to my physical body. I feel my body has been kept young and limber and pliable, because my mind is also of that attitude and working under those functional conditions. I find that the mind is the leader. I have a mind that can lead me out of problems or can lead me into them. I do not allow society to lead me. All I want to know is what is right and I'll do the right thing, even if I had to go alone and do it.

I don't think my family life and my home life was a good one. It was a mixed one. First of all, I had a good mother, she was a good healer, she assured me that everything was alright with me. While my father didn't believe in me. I was considered the black sheep. I couldn't do anything right, I was no good, and would never amount to any good.

That attitude by my father lit the spark in me. Which gave me the attitude, I'll show him, I'll do something he'll be proud of.

I've always been an achiever, and I'm not happy unless I do. I feel that that has been quite a compelling force within me. I used to travel and lecture with Napoleon Hill, who wrote *Think and Grow Rich*. What I learned from him is, no experience is a stumbling block. It should be used as a stepping stone. I feel that I have lived up to that motto. There have been other mentors. I would like to say Hippocrates was possibly the philosopher that I follow: that food is your medicine, medicine is your food. The next thought I got from him is that doctors will never understand disease until they understand the make-up of foods. I went along for years with that thought in mind. The second man that I looked to is Dr. V.G. Racine. He was a Norwegian homeopath. He was the one that told me that we can look to our foods as medicine. I went into that study with him and truly I believe that he was the greatest of all my mentors.

I was brought up in orthodox churches and I still believe in the orthodox way. I like to call myself a Christian, but I delved into all religions. I feel that the man that awakened me and gave me greater insight into my Christian feelings and Christian training was Manley Hall. He is a walking encyclopedia of information and philosophical thought.

I am very much aware that some people are so spiritual that they're no good here on earth. It must be a practical thing. I think because of my mother's training, that if you go alone it's perfectly alright. But on the other hand, I'm unafraid because I feel I tried to do it with the approval of God. I'm not off on the seventh cloud. It's a matter of working with the planet, the planet's activities: the sun, air, water, our foods. If I can see this as God and nature, I work close to that and I feel that is the secret of my work. I come back and give you what I would call a more godly outlook, a more godly path to follow, a more natural path to follow. I tried to make this God an active thing, a planetary thing, a breathing thing.

Christ said that he was all things unto all men. When he was with the farmer, he talked about the power of the mustard seed. When he was with the fishermen, he talked about fishers of men. I follow those postulates. I follow the Christ in that respect because he was a healer. I'm interested in healing, whether it be physically, mentally or spiritually. That's how I view myself.

I felt like I was getting old around the age of 40, and I'd read a book on how to live to be 100. I started reading it and then I thought I'd better meet the author. I find out he was only 26 years old, and I thought this isn't the man I should listen to. So I started my travels to all the old men. I probably visited more old men that anyone else I know. I learned a lot of things for the good of my health. One of them came from a man, 153. His name was Gasonov, a Russian. I asked him, "what rules do you follow for living so long?" He says, "well, I didn't know I was going to live so long, so I have no rules." And that kind of put me in my place. We have so many social ideas, so many ideas of growing old. I went on in further to find out that all the old people seemed to have no inhibitions, they don't have any hostilities within them. They all had wonderful ideas. Out of all these things I've learned, I used them as the basis of my work, was being natural, pure, and whole. If you look at all the things that are being separated these days, we're getting into trouble because one man's got something better than another man. It's all fragmented living.

I used to hemorrhage blood from my lungs at the age of 18. My mother died of tuberculosis and consumption at the age of 29. I was told it runs in the family. Somehow or another I was determined to break the cycle. In my travels to over 60 countries, I've learned to take care of and heal myself. I'm going into my 83rd year in better health now than I was at 18. I believe my early problem was the stimulus that made me seek out advice and a solution. It gave me an interest into all the people of the world, and to get the best ideas.

I keep working because I feel that's one of the secrets of keeping the body well. Personally, from my studies, I feel that the brain is the greatest metabolizer and the one thing that makes your body well, active, and productive. When the brain dies out, the body dies out also. First of all, life is filled in the brain. And like a lady asked me the other day, "how old are you?" And I said, "how old do you think I am?" And she said, "well, how old do you feel?" And I began to feel for my age and I had no feeling. There is no age feeling there. The age feeling is in the brain itself.

I think that there's been a lot of discrimination against some of my thinking and in some of my work. I think that I have been just about ten years ahead of my detractors. I was more determined in developing my philosophy, recognizing that anything new is automatically opposed. I just had to develop the patience and wait for them to understand and catch up. I see myself as a pioneer, and they don't want to take anything more than just what they can understand. They are not open to other newer thinking. But it has taught me a lesson, I need them too. I learned one thing, you can only help a person one step above where he is.

Aging is natural. One of the things that impressed me when I met some of these old men that were above 100, was that they become counselors in the town. I don't think in our culture we live long enough to give the next generation the advice and the counseling that they should have. We're cut off from our ultimate potential before our time. The mind never grows old unless you allow it. Nothing can ever happen to you unless you give it your consent. Resentment and resistance will kill you before your time. We have to take things as they come, but you must continue to be interested in life. You must be interested in creativity. You must be able to construct constantly. In other words, it's like a child. Never give him a finished toy. Always give him something he has to build, something he has to work. You have to consider balance. You can't expect sweet thoughts with a sour stomach. And you can't have a good stomach unless there's joy in the mind. You'll find out that you can create a sour stomach with hateful thoughts.

I feel the reason some people age well and other don't is that they haven't conquered their hostilities. We should let things unravel and unfold naturally. Fighting inhibits things from flowing through us that are good. As one our presidents said, "we'll have peace even if we have to fight for it." I mean, I don't think you can have peace and fight for it at the same time. My philosophy is illustrated in the saying "it's only fools that argue but it's wise men that counsel."

I'm sure I'm not going to live long enough physically to do all that I want to do. I am just loaded mentally with things that should be accomplished. I would like to see a better construction for society, such as better health, better and lasting marriages, a better feeling about an individual's work, and a better outlook about life above all things.

I feel that people appreciate me because they feel better after they've met me. I feel that it is definitely a calling. I've had people who just want to talk to me for a minute. They have said that it meant more to them than anything. I have had people say I saved their lives. I don't save lives. I make them feel better, they then get the ball and carry it themselves.

Mary Ann Wright

CHAPTER THIRTY-TWO

Mary Ann Wright

As the Ambassador of Peace and the Angel of the Poor, Mary Ann Wright has been recognized by thousands of people ranging from former President Reagan, to Menachem Begin, to California Governor George Deukmejian. Her sincere dedication, love, and commitment to God, has directed her life over the past 11 years to feed and clothe the poor and homeless from Northern California and Mexico, to even in a small village in Africa where plans are underway for a school for under-privileged children, and a homeless shelter to accommodate 300 people.

Mother right has received numerous acclamations: as a guest on several talk shows, and the subject of numerous magazine, newspaper articles, and radio shows. Her honors include Oakland's Mother of the Year in 1989, Hospitality Hostess for the Amateur Athletic Union for the Olympic Games throughout the World, and spokesperson for the Church of God in Christ in local and nation events. In addition, she has been honored by California State Senators and Oakland city officials, including the proclamation of July 11, 1989 as Mary Ann Wright Day for the City of Oakland.

———— ❖ ————

My mother died when I was five, I'm the third child of six. I was only 14 when I got married. I never went to school. Even as a little girl, I really had it in the back of my mind that I wanted to do something extraordinary. I always wanted to be a public speaker, but I couldn't even read or write. It's just something that was inside of me. I just wanted to do something for humanity.

I was born in New Orleans, Louisiana. Then my father moved from New Orleans to Darlington, Louisiana. We moved to the country and became farmers. I had some beautiful parents. My father is still alive. He's 94. My grandmother on my mother's side was an outstanding woman in her community. She wanted nothing less than the best for her grandchildren and her children. In my estimation she was one of the most outstanding women of her time. Consequently, I grew up with a positive self image and confidence in my abilities.

All of my life I have been a Christian. I became a Christian when I was 11 years old. I've always had charity in my heart to help people. Even when we didn't have enough for our family, we divided the little bit that we did have to help others. It was 1980 when the Lord awakened me in the middle of the night and said, feed the hungry. I said, "feed the hungry?" I've been feeding the hungry all of my life, but not in His manner, like what we are doing now, a whole lot of people at one time. We've always been able to share with people here and there. But here, it's hundreds and thousands of people that we're doing it for.

I got busy on that same day, and went to the produce markets at Jack London Square. I asked for a sack of beans, a sack of potatoes, some fruit or whatever they had. We wanted to have a Christmas dinner for the homeless, and the hungry people on the street. Some merchants said yes and some said no. We had more that said yes than said no. It's kind of hard to say no to me because I just won't take no for an answer. I let them know that it's an honest thing that we're asking, and it's not something that we're begging for. I was not doing that to make a profit.

I get personal satisfaction from doing the things that we're doing for the people we are doing it for. It makes me feel good to know that the Lord has allowed this to be his handiwork. I'm just an instrument. The Lord called me to do it, and I'm his vessel that's doing what the Lord says to do. When you see four and five hundred people eat with dignity, it is heartwarming. This is what we've been doing in the park for 11 years. You see how fulfilling it is to them, they are so relaxed and grateful, and then you stand back and say, "Lord, look at the people who wouldn't have had anything today if we had not come." It makes me feel good to know that the Lord has given me the strength to come out and feed the people. This experience has made me stronger in my resolve.

If the spirit of God had not called me to this work, I'd have fallen by the wayside a long time ago. Seeing me feeding the hungry in the park, that's just one little scene. But it's getting it together and working almost 24 hours a day. Sometimes I sleep in a chair at night dead from exhaustion, although it's the greatest satisfaction that I ever had and it's the greatest work that I've ever done. I'm glad that I got the call to do it.

I have 12 children: 6 boys, 6 girls, 30 grandchildren, and 19 great grandchildren, and I raised 9 foster boys from the Youth Authority along with my children. When I look back on life, I wanted education so badly. I wanted to be the type of person that maybe I could go to the White House, work in the White House. I always wanted that. It was in the back of my mind. But since I didn't accomplish that in my youth, my children have fulfilled my spiritual and inner being. I love my family. I stuck with them through thick and thin, and I had to raise them as a single parent. My children were more important to me than anything. I had to survive to take care of them. I've never let anything come between my children and me. What I conveyed to them at all times is education is very important and I want you to get what your mom didn't have.

Think about the less fortunate people in hospitals and nursing homes with major problems. Those people, if they just had the opportunity that we had, they would be throwing up their hands, walking and praising God. We have to be thankful when we really take a look at others with mental and physical handicaps. I'm glad that the creator created me in the image that he did. I'm a people's person. I don't see black and white. I don't see colors. I see human beings. I just see people as they are. I love people, and I'm glad. It makes me feel good to know that I can smile. Maybe I may not feel like smiling, but I can smile, and I've asked the Lord to make me what he would have me to be.

We are trying now to get a shelter for the homeless. We want to get a shelter for the mothers and their babies to get them off the ground. We've got so many out there with no place to go, it makes my heart sad. We have not yet received a grant of any kind. We hope that the Lord will touch somebody's heart and we will get our donations. I have a lady who's been sending me five dollars for about six years. It means more to me, that five dollars, then somebody who'll send 50 dollars once a year. That's the way I feel about it.

I never think about age. All of my life, coming up as a young person I always said I'd never get old, age would come but I would never get old. I've never used any dye in my hair, I've forbidden that down through the years. I said, I want to get old gracefully, age gracefully, but I won't get old. I'm 69 but my attitude is 35.

I told my children, whoever's in charge in the organization, please don't let the work die when I die. We don't want it to be like Martin Luther King. I'm just making that statement because soon after he was gone, everything that he did, it all died down. When I look back on life, the Lord has done so many beautiful things for me. Now I feel like I have not lost anything from my youth, my childhood up to this day. I feel like the Lord has fulfilled my life. The things that I thought I missed, I have not missed, because I have accomplished everything that I really wanted to. I've been to the White House twice. I think a lot of time we let ourselves get into a state of feeling sorry for ourselves about the things that we desire in life. But you have to make the best of life. One day at a time. We can't think about tomorrow because tomorrow is not promised to us. The day is the day that the Lord has made for us, we're going to glory and enjoy this day.

Epilogue

I found that successful aging is by no means an accident. The information from these interviews can have wide applications to people of all ages, especially in the area of parenting. A large percentage of the participants had supportive parent(s) that helped develop their child's interests, or parents who did not impede the development of their child's individual interests. This approach to child rearing ultimately helped to foster the development of confidence in instinctual judgement at an early age. The implications are that as a child enters a particular stage of development, they have had years of positive reenforcement with respect to their interests, and confidence in their instincts. This, in turn, finds fruition in later years as they become confident, self-realized adults. The exploring and expanding of personal interests can be the basis for a life full of challenges, self-generating creativity, and success.

A large percentage of the interviewees were also found to have positively responded to strong, grounding home environments. That is to say, they each seemed to have parents who, while maintaining their didactic roles, also allowed time to counsel and encourage their children to grow and learn from their own efforts and experiences. Additionally, it also appears that to most respondents work was not modeled as an activity to be completed solely as a matter of necessity, but respected for what it could provide the individual emotionally. All of the people interviewed continue to thrive on work even though they need not work for a living. Another important factor that seemed common to all was that maintaining good health was a very important factor if one expected to age well.

Simply put, the foundations provided by the family translated into a solid, living, value system which has served each of them very well through the years. Their parents not only loved, respected and supported them, they held them accountable for their behavior and encouraged qualitative decision-making while demonstrating the relationship between the power of choices and the ability to extract all that life had to offer. They taught their children that they matter, and must always take control of their lives.

This is certainly a far cry from the family-farm system currently in place in our society today: the fragmented value-instruction of our children through such media as the schools, television, and the government. The results of this survey speak to a fundamental value system which is sadly lacking in our society today, and without which we seem to go through the motions of working, loving, respecting, and even playing.

The men and women I interviewed seem to have come to terms with life and dispelled a good number of the common misconceptions of aging. They seem to have given themselves permission to be who they are, instead of what others perceived them to be. Many of them view life as a continuum of learning experiences. They care about themselves and their fellow human beings. They love life so much they are willing to continue to work for the experience of it. They demonstrate that to create, no matter what the product is, they must put more in than they take out, and through that experience make a tangible difference for themselves and others.

In reviewing the research, there is a tremendous amount of inbred ageism in our society. The interviews dispelled some of the common myths:

- No need to start thinking about aging until your 65.
- Growing old means growing sick and helpless.
- Most older people are dependent and cannot live alone.
- Aging for men and women is pretty much the same.
- Sex doesn't sizzle after 60.
- Older people are unproductive.
- Older people are unattractive.

Creativity, and the factors that inhibit or enhance intellectual and artistic achievement in old age, have been especially neglected, as stated by The National Council on Aging.[15] The achievement of famous artists, writers, scientist, have shown that, while there are many individual exceptions, major contributions usually are made in the early, rather than the later decades of adulthood. It is not known to what extent social factors in old age can be altered to maintain creativity and productivity.

Notes

1. Comfort, Alex. *A Good Age*. New York: Crown Publishers, Inc. 1976.
2. "Madison Avenue Underestimates the Over-50 Market," *San Francisco Chronicle,* April 19, 1990.
3. Cousins, Norman. *Anatomy of An Illness*; Norton Publishers, Inc. 1979.
4. Lobsenz, Norman. "Why Do We Keep On Working?" *Parade Magazine,* Sept. 14, 1986, pp. 8-9.
5. Pratt, Fran. *Education for Aging: A Teacher's Sourcebook.* 1981.
6. *Aging Annual Edition.* Fifth Edition. Gilford: Dushkin Publishing Group. 1987.
7. "Longevity," *San Diego Union*: Currents Section Jan. 12, 1987, pp. 1,5.
8. "Human Potential," *San Diego Union*: Currents Section, Jan. 15 1987, pp. 1,5.
9. "Buck Center for Research in Aging," *Health Span*, Volume 1 No. 2 Fall 1990, p. 2.
10. Neugarten, Bernice L., Robert J. Havighurst, and Sheldon S. Tobin. "The Measurement of Life Satisfaction." *The Journal of Gerontology*, Vol. 1, no. 6 (1961), pp. 134-143.
11. Terwilliger, Elizabeth. *Sights and Sounds of the Seasons.* Tiburon: Elizabeth Terwilliger Nature Education Foundation, 1979.
12. "A Rare Jewel In The Treasure Chest Of Life," Braunstein-Quay Gallery Card for Beatrice Wood. [c.1989].
13. *Help Yourself to Good Health: Meet Alice Faye.* Pfizer Pharmaceuticals, 1990.
14. "The Coach and His Companion: John Wooden," *Sports Illustrated,* April 3, 1989, p. 94.
15. United States, U.S. Department of Health and Human Services. "Sex Differences and Aging," White House Conference on Aging. 1981, pp. 1-3.

Bibliography

"Aging In America: Dignity or Despair?" San Francisco: Presbyterian Medical Center. [c. 1989], pp. 1-11.

Aging. 5th ed. Guilford, Conneticut: Dushkin Publishing Group, Inc., 1987.

"Aging: Can It Be Slowed." *Business Week,* Feb. 8, 1988, pp. 58-64.

Bouranim, Hara Ann. *Teaching and Learning About Age.* Framingham: Framingham State College, 1981.

"Carter Likes Popularity, Lacks Aspirations," *San Rafael Indepedent Journal,* April 29. 1990.

Chinen, Allan B. *In the Ever After: Fairy Tales and the Second Half of Life.* Wilmette: Chiron Publications, 1981.

Clark, Etta. *Growing Old is Not for Sissies: Portraits of Senior Athletes.* Corte Madera: Pomegranate Books, 1986.

Comfort, Alex. "Good-by to Ageism." *Modern Maturity,* February - March 1977, pp. 8-10-.

Dychtwald, Kenneth M. *Age Wave.* New York: Bantam Books, 1989.

Gardner, John. "Ethics Courses Needed Business Dean Told." *San Francisco Chronicle,* April 24, 1990.

Hehinger, Grace. "Ideas for Living," *Growing Old in America,* No. 22. 1977, pp. 27-29.

In Marin: The Magazine of the North Bay. March 1990.

Kimmel, Douglas C. *Adulthood and Aging.* New York: John Wiley & Sons, 1974.

Lekich, Kata. *The Polluted Pond: The Myth About Aging.* New York: Carlton Press, Inc., 1987.

Longevity: A Practical Guide to the Art and Science of Staying Young. August 1989.

Morgan, David G. "Aging and Longevity." A Seminar for Health Professionals. Feb. 25, 1990, pp. 1-15.

Neugarten, Bernice L., ed. *Middle Age and Aging.* Chicago: University of Chicago Press, 1968.

Painter, Charlotte, and Pamela Valois. *Gifts of Age: Portraits and Essays of 32 Remarkable Women.* San Francisco: Chronicle Books, 1985.

"Portraits by the Poet: Lawrence Ferlinghetti". *San Francisco Chronicle,* April 21, 1990.

Ryan, Michael. "Do The Best You Can With What You've Got." *Parade Magazine,* May 17, 1987, pp. 4-5.

Sheehy, Gail. *Passages: Predictable Crises of Adult Life.* New York: E.P. Dutton, 1974.

Smith, Hal and Lisa. *Human Development: Successful Aging.* Irvine: Concept Media, Inc., 1980.

Stearn, Marshall B. "The Relationship of Parent Effectiveness Training to Parent Attitudes, Parent Behavior, and Child Self-Esteem." Diss. U.S.I.U. San Diego, 1971.

Steward, Dana, and Jeaninne Lamb. *A Fine Age: Creativity as a Key to Successful Aging.* Little Rock: August House, 1984.

"The Aging Mind Proves Capable of Lifelong Growth." *New York Times,* February 21, 1984.

U.S. Department of Health and Human Services. *Aging Words: A Glossary on Health and Aging.* January 1986.

U.S. Department of Health and Human Services. National Institute on Aging. *Special Report on Aging.* 1980.

U.S. Department of Health and Human Services. National Institute on Aging. *Age Pages.* November 1985.

United States. *Report of the Panel on Behavioral and Social Sciences Research.* U.S. Department of Health, Education, and Welfare, 1980.

Index

ORDER FORM

Park West Publishing Company
P.O. Box 1502, Sausalito, CA 94966

Please send me the following book(s) by
Marshall B. Stearn, Ph.D.

SELF HYPNOSIS:
A Method of Improving Your Life

_____copies ($6.95 ea.)

DRINKING & DRIVING:
Know Your Limits/ Liabilities

_____copies ($7.95 ea.)

Name: _____

Address: _____

Ciity/State/Zip: _____

California Residents Please Add 6% Sales Tax

SHIPPING: $2.50 PER BOOK. IF PAID IN CANADIAN CURRENCY ADD $3.50 PER BOOK. IF LARGE QUANTITIES OF BOOKS DESIRED, CONTACT PARK WEST PUBLISHING CO. FOR TERMS (415) 388-3566

Subliminal Persuasion/Self Hypnosis Tapes
Cartridge or 8-Track Only $9.98

Side 1: The subliminal persuasion format is designed for use anywhere. Each suggestion is recorded just below the conscious awareness level, at a point where it reaches effectively the subconscious.

Side 2: The Self-Hypnosis format allows you to consciously hear the same message, providing balance and coordination with your subconscious. You now have unity of the mind in two dimensions.

001 ABORTION: THE AFTER EFFECTS	074 JOY OF EXERCISE
002 ABUSE HEALED	075 LEO
003 AGORAPHOBIA	076 LIBRA
004 AQUARIUS	077 LONELINESS
005 ARIES	078 LOSS of a LOVED ONE
006 ARTHRITIS PAIN RELIEF	079 LOWER BLOOD PRESSURE
007 ASTRAL PROJECTION	080 LOWERING CHOLESTEROL
008 BASEBALL-CATCHING	081 MEMORY IMPROVEMENT
009 BASEBALL-HITTING	082 MIGRAINE RELIEF
010 BASEBALL-PITCHING	083 MISCARRIAGE: THE AFTER EFFECTS
011 BE A BETTER BOWLER	084 MONEY PROSPERITY
012 BE POSITIVE	085 MY PARENTS MYSELF
013 BETTER TABLE TENNIS	086 NATURAL BUST ENLARGEMENT
014 BETTER TENNIS	087 OPERATION BEFORE and AFTER
015 BIRTH SEPARATION	088 OVERCOMING PROCRASTINATION
016 BODY BUILDING	089 PAIN RELIEF
017 CANCER	090 PAINLESS DENTISTRY
018 CAPRICORN	091 PARALLEL LIVES-SEPARATE SELVES
019 CHAKRA MEDITATION	092 PAST LIFE REGRESSION
020 CHANNELING YOUR HIGHER SELF	093 PAST LIFE THERAPY (cause & effect)
021 CODEPENDENCE to SELF DISCOVERY	094 PEACE OF MIND
022 CONCENTRATION	095 PISCES
023 CREATIVE THINKING	096 PREMENSTRUAL SYNDROME
024 CREATIVE WRITING	097 PROBLEM SOLVING
025 DEATH & DYING	098 PSYCHIC HEALING
026 DEVELOP ENTHUSIASM	099 PSYCHIC PROJECTION
027 DEVELOP PSYCHIC ABILITIES	100 RACQUETBALL
028 DIVORCE NO	101 RECAPTURE YOUTHFUL VIGOR
029 DIVORCE YES	102 REKINDLE the ROMANCE (SPICE)
030 EFFECTIVE SPEAKING	103 RELATIONSHIP REPROGRAMMING
031 FACIAL TIC	104 RELAXATION
032 FASTER READING	105 RELIEF of BACK PAIN
033 FEAR of CLOSED in PLACES	106 RELIEVE STRESS & ANXIETY
034 FEAR of CROWDS	107 REMOVAL of WARTS
035 FEAR of DEATH	108 RUNNING/ JOGGING
036 FEAR of DRIVING	109 SAGGITARIUS
037 FEAR of FAILURE	110 SCORPIO
038 FEAR of FLYING	111 SELF CONFIDENCE (SELF IMAGE)
039 FEAR of HEIGHTS	112 SELF-HEALING
040 FEAR of SUCCESS	113 SELF-HYPNOSIS
041 FEAR of WATER	114 SEXUAL ABUSE (PERSONAL)
042 FREEDOM FROM ACNE	115 SKIING WITH THE WIND
043 FREEDOM FROM ALLERGIES	116 SO, YOUR OUT OF A JOB?
044 FREEDOM FROM DRUGS	117 STOMACH PROBLEMS
045 FREEDOM FROM GUILT	118 STOP BED WETTING (ENURESIS)
046 FREEDOM FROM SEXUAL GUILT	119 STOP BEING ANGRY
047 FREEDOM FROM WORRY	120 STOP DRINKING
048 GEMINI	121 STOP LOSS OF HAIR
049 MORE JOY OUT OF SEX (M)	122 STOP NAIL BITING
050 MORE JOY OUT OF SEX (F)	123 STOP SMOKING
051 GETTING the RAISE you DESERVE	124 STOP STUTTERING
052 GOAL SETTING	125 SUBCONSCIOUS SALES POWER
053 GOOD STUDY HABITS	126 SUCCESSFUL RETIREMENT
054 HANDLING DISAPPOINTMENT	127 TAKING EXAMS
055 HAVING A BABY	128 TALENTS/ABILITIES FROM PAST LIFE
056 HEALING ABUSED: PAST LIFE	129 TAPERING OFF SMOKING
057 HEALING RESTORED	130 TAURUS
058 HOUSEKEEPING WITH LOVE	131 THE TWELVE STEPS TO FREEDOM
059 HOW TO ATTRACT LOVE	132 THUMB SUCKING
060 HOW TO BE A GREAT GOLFER	133 TIME MANAGEMENT
061 HOW TO BE POPULAR	134 TIME TRAVELER
062 HOW TO HANDLE CRITICISM	135 TOUCH ME
063 HYPERACTIVE CHILDREN	136 UP FROM DEPRESSION
064 I AM JEALOUS	137 VIETNAM VETERAN
065 I FREE YOU FROM JEALOUSY	138 VIRGO
066 I LOVE MY BODY (F)	139 VISUALIZE AURA READING
067 I LOVE MY BODY (M)	140 WALK-DON'T JOG
068 I WANT TO BE HAPPY	141 WEIGHT-GAIN
069 IMAGING	142 WEIGHT-LOSS
070 IMPOTENT NO MORE	143 WHERE IS MY CHILD (NATURAL PARENT)
071 IMPROVING VISION	144 WHERE IS MY PARENT (ADOPTED CHILD)
072 INNER DANCE OF MARTIAL ARTS	145 WILL POWER
073 INSOMNIA	146 WORLD PEACE
	147 YOU AND YOUR CHILD

CONTINUED ON NEXT PAGE WITH ORDER FORM

ORDER FORM

CIRCLE CORRESPONDING NUMBERS FROM LIST

001 002 003 004 005 006 007 008 009 010 011 012 013 014
015 016 017 018 019 020 021 022 023 024 025 026 027 028
029 030 031 032 033 034 035 036 037 038 039 040 041 042
043 044 045 046 047 048 049 050 051 052 053 054 055 056
057 058 059 060 061 062 063 064 065 066 067 068 069 070
071 072 073 074 075 076 077 078 079 080 081 082 083 084
085 086 087 088 089 090 091 092 093 094 095 096 097 098
099 100 101 102 103 104 105 106 107 108 109 110 111 112
113 114 115 116 117 118 119 120 121 122 123 124 125 126
127 128 129 130 131 132 133 134 135 136 137 138 139 140
141 142 143 144 145 146 147

CHECK: ☐ **Cassette**   OR   ☐ **8-Track**

_____ **tapes at $9.98 per tape**
no of tapes

Subtotal $ _____

Shipping & Handling $ ___2.50___

6% Sales Tax For CA Residents $ _____

TOTAL $ _____

Date _____

Signature_____

Name (printed)_____

Address _____

City/State/Zip _____

MAIL YOUR ORDER TO:
WEST PUBLISHING • POST OFFICE BOX 1502 • SAUSALITO, CA 94966